A QUICK COURSE IN

EXCEL 5

For Windows

Computer

training

books

for busy

people

JOYCE COX

JOYCE COUSINEAU

PUBLISHED BY
Online Press Inc.
14320 NE 21st Street, Suite 18
Bellevue, WA 98007
(206) 641-3434, (800) 854-3344

Publisher's Cataloging in Publication
(Prepared by Quality Books Inc.)

Cox, Joyce.
    A quick course in Excel 5 for Windows / Joyce Cox, Joyce
Cousineau.
    p. cm.
    Includes index.
    ISBN 1-879399-28-8

    1. Microsoft Excel for Windows. 2. Business--Computer programs.
3. Electronic spreadsheets.   I. Cousineau, Joyce.   II. Title.

HF5548.4.M523C68 1994   650'.0285'5369
                               QBI93-22122
                                         93-086431
                                         CIP

Printed and bound in the United States of America.

1 2 3 4 5 6 7 8 9 X L X L 3 2 1 0

DEDICATION

To our friend and colleague Pat Kervran (aka Peter Karnov)
with fond memories

Contents

1

Building a Simple Worksheet

What you will learn...

Enter numeric values as text

Make headings bold and centered

Adjust column widths to accommodate long entries

Date	Invoice Number	Salesperson		Amount of Sale
3-Jan-94	4739AA	Crux, Jamie		83456.23
4-Jan-94	943200	Olderon, Sam		90875.56
10-Jan-94	8488AA	Karnov, Peter		63456.83
17-Jan-94	4398AA	Smite, Karlina		42356.07
3-Feb-94	4945AA	Crux, Tad		65643.9
8-Feb-94	825600	Furban, Wally		123456.45
14-Feb-94	846500	Ladder, Larry		67345.23
2-Mar-94	4409AA	Karnov, Peter		145768.34
11-Mar-94	8867AA	Crux, Jamie		43256.23
23-Mar-94	875600	Ladder, Larry		11256.9
30-Mar-94	479300	Furban, Wally		85345

Assign a different date format

Insert entire columns or rows

You're probably sitting at your computer, anxious to start crunching numbers. But before we start, we need to cover some basics, such as how to enter text and numbers, save files, move around a worksheet, edit and format entries, and print the results of your labors. After we discuss a few fundamentals, you'll easily be able to create the worksheets and charts we cover in the rest of the book.

We assume that you've already installed Windows 3.1 or later and Excel 5 on your computer. We also assume that you've worked with Windows before and that you know how to start programs, move windows, choose commands from menus, highlight text, and so on. If you are a Windows novice, we recommend that you take a look at *A Quick Course in Windows*, another book in the Quick Course series, which will help you quickly come up to speed.

To follow the instructions in this book, you must be using a mouse. Although it is theoretically possible to work in Windows and Excel using just the keyboard, we would not wish this fate on anyone, and most of our instructions involve using a mouse. Occasionally, however, when it is easier or faster to use the keyboard, we give the keyboard equivalent of the mouse action.

Let's get going. With the DOS prompt (C:\>) on your screen, start Windows by typing *win* and pressing Enter. Then in Windows, start Excel by double-clicking the Excel icon in its group window. (Unless you specified during installation that you wanted to assign Excel to a different group, you will probably find the icon in the Microsoft Office group window.)

If this is the first time you've started Excel, you see a Quick Preview screen that gives you the opportunity to take one of four electronic get-acquainted tours. If you're not interested in seeing any of these previews before you get started, click the Return To Microsoft Excel button in the bottom right corner of the screen.

Getting Oriented

When you start Excel for the first time, your screen looks something like this:

Clicking and double-clicking

Clicking is a simple matter of pressing and releasing the mouse button once. To double-click, you *quickly* click the mouse button twice. If double-clicking doesn't produce the anticipated result, try again, this time clicking a little faster.

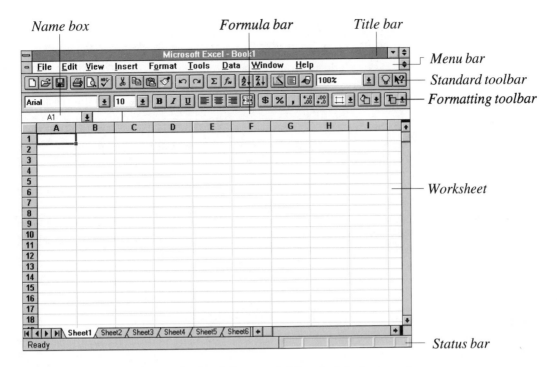

At the top of the screen is the Microsoft Excel *title bar*, and below that is the *menu bar*, from which you choose commands. Below the menu bar are the *Standard toolbar* and the *Formatting toolbar*, which put a host of often-used tools within reach. (These toolbars are just two of 13 toolbars available in Excel.) Below the Formatting toolbar is the *formula bar*, in which you enter the values (text and numbers) and formulas that you'll use in your worksheet.

Taking up the majority of the screen is the blank *worksheet*, which as you can see, is laid out in a grid of *columns* and *rows* like the ledger paper used by accountants. There are 256 columns, lettered A through IV, and 16,384 rows, numbered 1 through 16384. The rectangle at the junction of each column and row is called a *cell*. To identify each of the 4 million plus cells on the worksheet, Excel uses an *address*, or *reference*, that consists of the letter at the top of the cell's column and the number at the left end of its row. For example, the reference of the cell in the top left corner of the worksheet is A1. The *active cell*—the one you are working with—is designated on the worksheet by a heavy border. Excel displays the reference of the active cell in the *name box* at the left end of the formula bar.

Mouse pointer shapes

The mouse pointer takes on different shapes depending on where it is on the screen. For example, the pointer is an arrow when it is over the title bar, the menu bar, or a toolbar; an I-beam when it is over the formula bar; a double-headed arrow when it is over a column or row header; and a cross when it is over the worksheet.

The worksheet you see on your screen is just one *sheet* in the current file, which is called a *workbook*. By default, each new workbook contains 16 sheets. However, a single workbook file can contain as many as 255 sheets, named Sheet1 through Sheet255. You can have several types of sheets in one workbook, including worksheets; chart sheets, which chart your data; and macro sheets, which store automated ways of manipulating the data or the workbook. This workbook format allows you to store related data on separate sheets but in a single file.

At the bottom of the screen, the *status bar* displays useful information about commands and toolbar buttons and the status of keys, such as whether Caps Lock is turned on.

An Overview of Workbooks

For each sheet in a workbook, Excel displays a *tab*, like a file folder tab, above the status bar at the bottom of the screen. These tabs are handy for moving from sheet to sheet. Let's see how to use them to move around the workbook:

Displaying sheets

1. Click the Sheet2 tab. Excel displays that sheet.

2. Next, click the Sheet6 tab. Excel displays Sheet6 and moves the tabs to the left so that the Sheet7 tab is visible.

3. Keep clicking the rightmost tab until Sheet16 is displayed.

An easier way to move between the sheets is to use the *tab scrolling buttons* to the left of the tabs. The two outer buttons take you to the beginning and end of the tab display, and the two inner buttons move you one tab at a time in the direction of the button's arrow.

Scrolling tabs

1. Click the leftmost button. Excel displays the tabs for the first six sheets but does not change the displayed sheet.

2. Click the rightmost button. Excel displays the last set of tabs, with the tab for Sheet 16 still highlighted.

3. Try the other buttons to see how they work, and finish by selecting Sheet1.

Entering Text

Most worksheets consist of blocks of text and numbers in table format on which you can perform various calculations. To make your worksheets easy to decipher, you usually enter text as column and row headings that describe the associated entries. Let's try entering a few headings now:

1. With cell A1 selected, type *Date*. As you type, the text appears in both the cell and the formula bar, and a blinking insertion point in the cell tells you where the next character you type will be inserted. A Cancel button (✗), Confirm button (✓), and Function Wizard button (*fx*) appear between the text and name box. Meanwhile, the indicator in the status bar changes from Ready to Enter, because the text that you have typed will not be recorded in cell A1 until you "enter" it.

2. Click the Confirm button to complete the entry. Excel enters the Date heading in cell A1, and the indicator changes to Ready. Notice that the entry is left-aligned in its cell. Unless you tell Excel to do otherwise, it always left-aligns text.

3. Click cell B1 to select it. The reference displayed in the name box changes from A1 to B1.

4. Type *Invoice Number*, but instead of clicking the Confirm button to enter the heading in the cell, press the Right Arrow key. Excel completes the entry in cell B1 and selects cell C1.

5. Type *Salesperson* and press the Right Arrow key.

6. Now enter one more heading. In cell D1, type *Amount of Sale* and click Confirm to complete the entry. Here's how the newly entered row of headings looks in the worksheet:

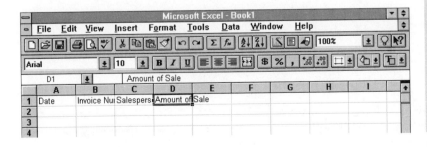

Entering headings

Correcting mistakes

If you make a mistake, you can click the cell containing the error and simply type the new entry. If you want to correct part of an entry, click its cell and press F2, or double-click the cell, so that you can edit the entry directly in the cell. You can then press Home or End to move the insertion point to the beginning or end of the entry and press Right Arrow or Left Arrow to move the insertion point forward or backward one character. Press Backspace to delete the character before the insertion point or Delete to delete the character after the insertion point. Then type the correction and click the Confirm button.

Long text entries ————————▶

Notice that the headings in cells B1, C1, and D1 are too long to fit in their cells. Until you entered the Salesperson heading in cell C1, the Invoice Number heading spilled over into C1, just as Amount of Sale now spills over from D1 into E1. After you entered the Salesperson heading, Excel truncated Invoice Number so that you could read the heading in C1. The Invoice Number and Salesperson headings are still intact, however. (If you're skeptical, click either cell and look at the formula bar.) Later in this chapter, you'll learn how to adjust column widths to accommodate long entries (see page 27).

That completes the column headings. Now let's turn our attention to the rest of the table. We'll skip the Date and Invoice Number columns for now and enter the names of a few salespeople in last-name/first-name order in column C.

1. Click cell C2 and type *Crux, Jamie*.

2. Instead of clicking the Confirm button, press the Down Arrow key. Excel completes the entry in C2 and selects cell C3.

3. In cell C3, type *Olderon, Sam* and press the Down Arrow key to complete the entry and move to cell C4.

4. Next, type the following names in the Salesperson column, pressing the Down Arrow key after each one:

C4	Karnov, Peter
C5	Smite, Karlina
C6	Crux, Tad
C7	Furban, Wally
C8	Ladder, Larry
C9	Karnov, Peter
C10	Crux, Jamie
C11	Ladder, Larry
C12	Furban, Wally

Entering Numbers as Text

Now let's enter the invoice numbers in column B. Normally, you will want Excel to treat invoice numbers—and social security numbers, part numbers, phone numbers, and other numbers that are used primarily for identification—as text rather than as values on which you might want to perform calculations. If the "number" includes not only the digits 0 through 9 but also letters and other characters (such as hyphens), Excel usually recognizes it as a text. However, if the number consists of only digits and you want Excel to treat it as text, you have to explicitly tell Excel to do so.

For demonstration purposes, assume that your company has two regional offices, East and West. Both offices use invoice numbers with six characters. Invoices generated by the East office consist of four digits followed by the letters AA, and those generated by the West office consist of six digits that end with 00 (two zeros). Follow these steps to see how Excel treats these invoice numbers:

1. Click cell B2, type *4739AA* and press Down Arrow. This invoice number consists of both digits and letters, so Excel treats the entry as text and left-aligns it.

2. In cell B3, which is now active, type *943200* and click the Confirm button. This invoice number consists of only digits, so Excel treats the entry as a value and right-aligns it.

How do you tell Excel to treat an entry that consists of only digits as text? You begin the entry with a single quote mark ('). Follow these steps:

Using single quote marks

1. In cell B3, type *'943200* and press Enter. (When you type the new entry, Excel overwrites the old entry.) Because of the single quote mark, Excel recognizes the new entry as text.

2. Enter these invoice numbers as text in the indicated cells, preceding those that end in 00 with a single quote mark:

B4	8488AA
B5	4398AA
B6	4945AA
B7	'825600
B8	'846500
B9	4409AA
B10	8867AA
B11	'875600
B12	'479300

Turn the page to see the results.

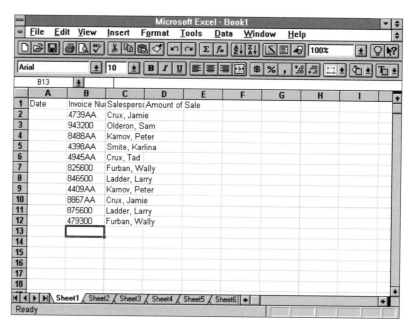

Long numeric values

Excel allows a long text entry to overflow into an adjacent empty cell and truncates the entry only if the adjacent cell also contains an entry. However, Excel treats a long numeric value differently. If Excel displays pound signs (#) instead of the value you entered, the value is too large to display in the cell. By default, values are displayed in scientific notation, and values with many decimal places might be rounded. For example, if you enter 12345678912345 in a standard width cell (which holds 8.43 characters), Excel displays 1.23E+13 (1.23 times 10 to the 13th power). And if you enter 123456.789 in a standard width cell, Excel displays 123456.8. In both cases, Excel leaves the underlying value unchanged, and you can widen the column to display the value in the format in which you entered it. (Adjusting the width of columns is discussed on page 27.)

Entering Values

As you have seen, entering numeric values is just as easy as entering text. Follow along with the next few steps as we enter the sales amounts in column D:

1. Click cell D2 to select the first cell in the Amount of Sale column, and type *83456.23*. Press Down Arrow to complete the entry, which Excel right-aligns in its cell.

2. Enter the following amounts in the indicated cells, pressing Down Arrow after each one:

D3	90875.56
D4	634568.30
D5	42356.07
D6	65643.90
D7	123456.45
D8	67345.23
D9	145768.34
D10	43256.23
D11	11256.90
D12	85345.00

Don't worry if Excel does not display these values exactly as you entered them. On page 47, we format these amounts so that they display as dollars and cents.

Entering Dates and Times

For a date or time to be displayed correctly, you must enter it "in format," meaning that you must enter it in a format that Excel recognizes as a date or time. Excel then displays the entry as you want it but stores it as a value so that you can conveniently perform date and time arithmetic. The following formats are recognized:

3/9/94	9:35 PM
9-Mar-94	9:35:43 PM
9-Mar	9:35
Mar-94	

Date and time formats

Two additional formats combine both date and time and take these forms:

3/9/94 9:35   3-9-94 9:35

Let's see how Excel handles different date formats:

1. Enter the following dates in the indicated cells, pressing the Down Arrow key after each one. Don't worry if Excel displays the dates differently from the way you enter them. Later, we'll come back and make sure all the dates appear in the same format.

A2	3-Jan-94
A3	1/4/94
A4	10-Jan-94
A5	17-Jan-94
A6	3-Feb-94
A7	2/8/94
A8	2/14/94
A9	3/2/94
A10	3/11/94
A11	23-Mar-94
A12	30-Mar-94

As you can see on the next page, you've now completed all the columns of this simple worksheet.

Date and time arithmetic

Each date you enter is internally recorded by Excel as a value that represents the number of days that have elapsed between that date and the base date of January 1, 1900, which is assigned the value 1. As a result, you can perform arithmetic with dates—for example, you can have Excel determine whether a payment is past due. Similarly, each time you enter is internally recorded as a decimal value that represents the portion of the day that has elapsed between that time and the base time of 12:00 midnight.

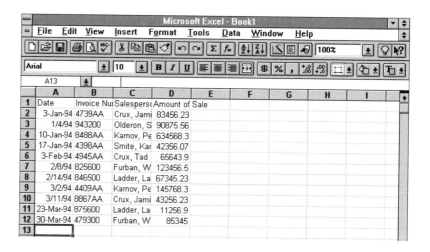

Moving Around

The fastest way to move around the worksheet is with the mouse. As you've seen, clicking any cell moves the cell pointer to that location and displays a new reference in the name box at the left end of the formula bar. To display parts of the worksheet that are currently out of sight, you can use the scroll bars, which function the same way as scroll bars in all Windows applications. Try this:

1. With cell A1 selected, click the arrows at the bottom of the vertical scroll bar and the right end of the horizontal scroll bar until cell P37 comes into view.

Jumping to cell A1 → 2. Press Ctrl+Home to jump back to cell A1.

As you just demonstrated, you can also use the keyboard to move around the worksheet. The keys you'll probably use most often are the four arrow keys, but as you gain more experience with Excel, you might find other keys useful. Here is a list of some of the navigation keys and what they do:

To do this...	Press...
Scroll down one window length	Page Down
Scroll up one window length	Page Up
Scroll right one window width	Alt+Page Down
Scroll left one window width	Alt+Page Up
Move to end of active area	Ctrl+End
Move to cell A1	Ctrl+Home

Another way to move around the worksheet is with the Go To command. Try this:

Jumping to a specific cell

1. Choose Go To from the Edit menu to display this dialog box:

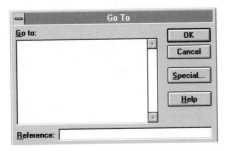

2. Type *Z46* in the Reference edit box and click OK. Immediately, Excel scrolls the worksheet and selects cell Z46.

3. Press Ctrl+Home to return to cell A1.

Selecting Ranges

Well, we've created a basic worksheet. But before we can show you some of the things you can do with it, we first need to discuss how to select blocks of cells, called *ranges*. Any rectangular block or blocks containing more than one cell is a range. A range can include two cells, an entire row or column, or the entire worksheet. Knowing how to select and work with ranges saves you time because you can apply formats to or reference the whole range, instead of dealing with each cell individually. *Range references* consist of the address of the cell in the top left corner of the rectangular block and the address of the cell in the bottom right corner, separated by a colon. For example, A1:B2 identifies the range that consists of cells A1, A2, B1, and B2.

Ranges

Range references

The simplest way to learn how to select ranges is to actually do it, so follow these steps:

1. Point to cell A1, hold down the left mouse button, and drag diagonally to cell D12 without releasing the button. Notice that the reference in the name box at the left end of the formula bar reads 12R x 4C, which indicates that you are selecting a range of cells 12 rows high by 4 columns wide.

Selecting more than one block

A range can consist of more than one block of cells. To select a multiblock range, select the first range, hold down the Ctrl key, select the next range, and so on.

2. Release the mouse button when the range A1:D12 is high-lighted. As you can see here, cell A1—the cell where you started the selection—is white, indicating that it is the active cell in the range.

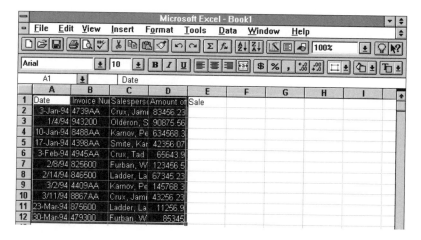

Next, try selecting ranges with the keyboard:

Selecting with the keyboard

1. Select cell B6, hold down the Shift key, press the Right Arrow key twice and the Down Arrow key twice, and release the Shift key. The range B6:D8 is selected.

2. Click anywhere on the worksheet to deselect the range.

Giving Excel Instructions

Now that you know how to select cells and ranges, let's quickly cover how you tell Excel what it should do with your selection.

Using Menus

You can give Excel instructions by choosing *commands* that are arranged in *menus* on the menu bar. Because this procedure is the same for all Windows applications, we assume that you are familiar with it and provide only a quick review here. If you are a new Windows user, we suggest that you spend a little time becoming familiar with the mechanics of menus, commands, and dialog boxes before proceeding.

Choosing commands

To choose a command from a menu, you first click the menu on the menu bar. When the menu drops down, you simply click the name of the command you want. To do the same thing with the keyboard, you can press the Alt key to activate the menu bar, press the underlined letter of the name of the menu, and then press the underlined letter of the command you want.

Some command names are followed by an arrowhead, indicating that a *submenu* will appear when you choose that command. You choose commands from submenus just like commands from regular menus.

Submenus

Some command names are followed by an ellipsis (...), indicating that you must supply more information before Excel can carry out the command. When you choose one of these commands, Excel displays a *dialog box*. Some dialog boxes have several tabs. You can display the options on a tab by clicking it. You give the information necessary to carry out a command by typing in an *edit box* or by selecting options from *lists* and clicking *check boxes* and *option buttons*. (All dialog boxes have a Help button that provides information about the dialog box, including how to complete its edit boxes and select its options.) You close the dialog box and carry out the command according to your specifications by clicking a *command button*—usually OK or Close. Clicking Cancel closes the dialog box and cancels the command. Other command buttons might be available to open other dialog boxes or to refine the original command.

Dialog boxes

Some command names are occasionally displayed in gray letters, indicating that you can't choose those commands. For example, the Paste command on the Edit menu appears in gray until you have used the Cut or Copy command.

As a short example of how to use menu commands and dialog boxes, follow these steps to apply a display format to the dates you entered in column A of your worksheet:

1. Use the mouse or keyboard to select the range A2:A12, which contains the dates.

2. Click Format on the menu bar to drop down the Format menu.

3. Click Cells to display the dialog box shown on the next page.

Help with commands

If you can't remember the name of the command you want to use, you can pull down each menu and press the Up Arrow and Down Arrow keys to highlight each command in turn. A brief description of the highlighted command appears in the window's status bar.

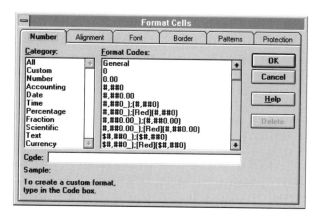

This dialog box contains six tabs for formatting different aspects of a cell, allowing you to handle all the formatting from this one dialog box. The first tab—Number—should be displayed. If it isn't, click it.

4. Click Date in the Category list.

5. Click d-mmm-yy in the Format Codes list. Then click OK to close the dialog box and apply the format to the selected cells.

6. Press Ctrl+Home to move to cell A1. Excel displays all the dates in the same format, as shown here:

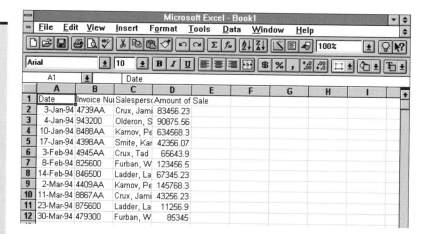

Accounting vs. currency formats

Excel provides four accounting formats and four currency formats that are parallel except for the location of the dollar signs in relation to the values. In accounting formats, the dollar sign is left-aligned in the cell, whereas the value is right-aligned. In currency formats, both the dollar sign and the value are right-aligned. All of these formats consist of two parts; the part preceding the semicolon applies to positive values and the part following the semicolon applies to negative values.

Using Shortcut Menus

Shortcut menus are context-sensitive menus that group together the commands used frequently with a specific type of object, such as a cell or a window element. You display the shortcut menu by pointing to the object and clicking the right mouse button. (From now on, we will refer to this action as *right-clicking*.) You can then choose a command from the menu in the usual way. We'll use shortcut menus whenever they are the most efficient method of giving Excel instructions.

← **Right-clicking**

Using Toolbars

Another way to give instructions is by clicking buttons on a toolbar. Excel comes with 13 built-in toolbars: Standard, Formatting, Query And Pivot, Chart, Drawing, TipWizard, Forms, Stop Recording, Visual Basic, Auditing, Workgroup, Microsoft, and Full Screen. You can customize these toolbars to suit your needs, and you can create your own toolbars. By default, Excel displays the Standard and Formatting toolbars, but you can display a different toolbar at any time. You can also move and resize toolbars. Simply click anywhere on the toolbar (except on a button), and drag it away from the top of the screen. The floating toolbar then acquires a title bar and borders, which you can use to move and resize the toolbar just like any window. Double-click the title bar to return the toolbar to its original position. The next time you move the toolbar, it returns to its previous resized shape. Try this:

1. Right-click anywhere on a toolbar to display a shortcut menu that lists some of the available toolbars, as shown here:

← **Displaying toolbars**

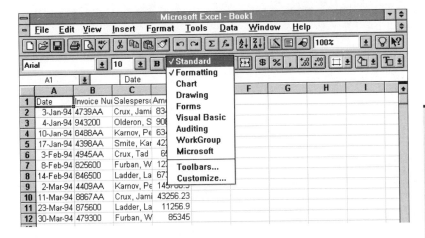

2. Choose Chart from the shortcut menu to display a floating Chart toolbar.

Help with toolbar buttons

A feature called *ToolTips* provides brief descriptions of all the toolbar buttons. When you move the mouse pointer over a button, ToolTips displays the button's name below the button and a description of the button's action in the status bar.

3. Double-click the toolbar's title bar to move it to the top of the screen, below the Formatting toolbar, as shown here:

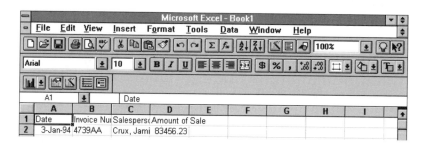

4. Point to the Chart toolbar and drag it from the toolbar area over the worksheet.

5. Click the close box (the box with the hyphen) at the left end of the toolbar's title bar to remove the toolbar from the screen.

Using Keyboard Shortcuts

If you and your mouse don't get along and you prefer to use the keyboard, you can access many Excel commands with keyboard shortcuts. You can display a list of these shortcuts by choosing Contents from the Help menu, clicking Reference Information, and then clicking Keyboard Guide. (For more information about Excel's Help system, see page 31.)

Saving Workbooks

Let's return to the workbook we are working with and save it for future use. As you'll see if you follow these steps, the first time you save a workbook, you must give its file a name:

1. Click the Save button. Because you have not yet assigned the workbook a name, Excel displays the Save As dialog box:

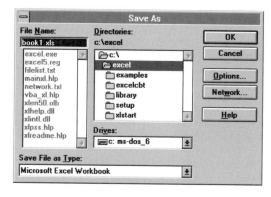

2. In the File Name edit box, type *invoices* to replace the suggested filename. There's no need to supply an extension because Excel automatically uses XLS to indicate that the file is an Excel workbook.

3. In the Directories list, double-click *examples* to indicate that you want to store the new workbook's file in the EXAMPLES subdirectory of the EXCEL directory.

4. Leave the other settings in the dialog box as they are for now, and click OK to carry out the command. Excel then displays this Summary Info dialog box:

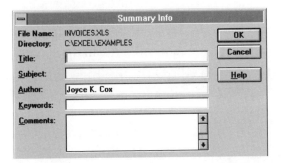

Excel automatically displays the Summary Info dialog box the first time you save a file. (You can display the dialog box at any time by choosing Summary Info from the File menu.) If you need to locate the INVOICES workbook later, you can use the Find File command on the File menu to search for files on your hard drive based on the information you enter in this dialog box. (If you don't anticipate using this method of finding files, you can tell Excel not to display this dialog box by choosing Options from the Tools menu, clicking the General tab, clicking the Prompt For Summary Info option to deselect it, and clicking OK.) For this example, we'll enter only a title and the author's name in the dialog box:

1. In the Title edit box, type *Invoice Log*.

2. If necessary, replace the entry in the Author edit box with your name, and click OK.

When you return to the worksheet, notice that the name INVOICES.XLS has replaced Book1 in the title bar.

Save options

Clicking the Options button in the Save As dialog box displays the Save Options dialog box. Selecting the Always Create Backup option causes Excel to create a copy of the existing version of the workbook before overwriting it with the new version. Excel gives the copy the extension BAK. Assigning a password in the Protection Password edit box tells Excel not to open the workbook until the password is entered correctly. Assigning a password in the Write Reservation Password edit box tells Excel to open a read-only version of the workbook if the password is not entered correctly. The read-only version can be altered but can be saved only with a different name. Selecting the Read-Only Recommended option tells Excel to warn users that the workbook should be opened as read-only, but does not prevent opening the workbook in the usual way. Other save options are available on the General tab of the dialog box that appears when you choose Options from the Tools menu. For example, you can specify a default directory for your workbooks in the Default File Location edit box.

Saving existing worksheets →

From now on, you can save this workbook by simply clicking the Save button. Excel then saves the workbook by overwriting the previous version with the new version. If you want to save the changes you have made to a workbook but preserve

Preserving the previous version →

the previous version, you can assign the new version a different name by choosing the Save As command from the File menu, entering the new filename, and clicking OK.

Editing Basics

In this section, we briefly cover some simple ways of revising worksheets so that in future chapters we can give general editing instructions without having to go into great detail.

Working with multiple worksheets →

Up to now you have been working with one worksheet. In the following examples we will copy data from one worksheet to another in the workbook. We will then split the window to display two different worksheets in the same workbook and move data between the worksheets. Being able to display more than one worksheet at a time can be very useful when you want to view the data in one while working in another.

Changing Entries

First let's see how to change individual entries. Glancing at the Amount of Sale column in Sheet1 of the INVOICES workbook, notice that the amount in cell D4 is suspiciously large compared with all the other amounts. Suppose you check this number and find to your disappointment that the amount should be 63456.83, not 634568.3. To correct the entry without having to retype the whole thing, follow these steps:

Direct cell editing →

1. Double-click cell D4 to select the cell and position an insertion point in the current entry.

2. Point between the 6 and 8 in the cell and click the left mouse button to reposition the insertion point. Then type a period (.).

3. Click between the second period and the 3 and press the Backspace key to delete the second period.

4. Press Enter to confirm the corrected entry.

You can also click a cell and press F2 to change an entry.

Copying Entries

You can copy an entry or group of entries anywhere within the same worksheet or in a different worksheet. Copy operations involve the use of two commands: Copy and Paste. You can choose these commands from the Edit menu, or you can click the equivalent buttons on the Standard toolbar. Follow these steps:

1. Select A1:D12 and click the Copy button or choose Copy from the Edit menu. Excel stores a copy of the entries in the selected range on the Windows Clipboard.

2. Select cell E1 and click the Paste button or choose Paste from the Edit menu. Excel assumes that the selected cell is the top left corner of the paste area and pastes the copied entries into E1:H12. (Notice that you don't have to select the entire paste area.)

Now try using Excel's shortcut menus:

1. Select cell F1 and then right-click to display this shortcut menu:

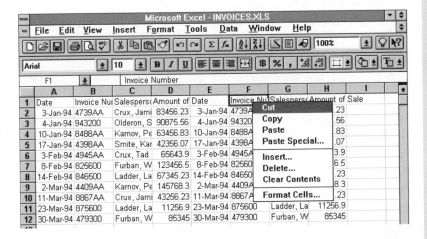

2. Choose Paste from the shortcut menu. Excel uses the selected cell as the top left corner of the paste area and, without warning, pastes the copied cells over the existing contents of cells F1:I12, as shown on the next page.

The Clipboard

The Windows Clipboard temporarily stores cut or copied data from all Windows applications. You can use it to transfer data from one document to another in the same application or from one application to another. Each item you cut or copy overwrites the previous item. Because the Clipboard is a temporary storage place, exiting Windows or turning off your computer erases any information stored there. To preserve information from one session to the next, you can save the contents of the Clipboard as a file by switching to Program Manager, double-clicking the Clipboard Viewer icon to display the Clipboard window, choosing Save As from the File menu, assigning the file a name, and clicking OK.

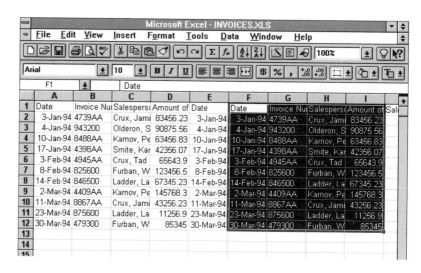

Cause for panic? Not at all. Excel's Undo command is designed for just such an occasion.

Undoing commands

3. Click the Undo button or choose Undo Paste from the Edit menu. Excel restores your worksheet to its prepaste status.

The copied information is still on the Clipboard, so let's make yet another copy, this time in Sheet2:

1. Click the Sheet2 tab to display that sheet.

2. With cell A1 selected, click the Paste button. Excel faithfully pastes in a copy of the range from Sheet1.

You can also use a simple mouse operation called *AutoFill* to copy and paste cells. Follow these steps:

1. With A1:D12 selected in Sheet2, move the pointer to the bottom right corner of the selected range.

2. When the pointer changes to a black cross, called the *fill handle*, hold down the left mouse button, and drag until the outline of the selection is over the range E1:H12.

3. Release the mouse button. Excel pastes a copy of the selected cells into the designated paste area.

4. Click the Sheet1 tab to return to Sheet1.

Copying and moving with the keyboard

You can use keyboard shortcuts to copy a range to the Clipboard and then paste it from the Clipboard into your worksheet. Select the range and press Ctrl+C. Then click the cell in the top left corner of the destination range and press Ctrl+V. To move the range instead of copying it, follow the same procedure but use Ctrl+X instead of Ctrl+C.

The result of dragging a copy is similar to using the Copy and Paste buttons or the equivalent commands, except that Excel doesn't place a copy of the selected range on the Clipboard. Because dragging requires that you hold down the mouse button, it's probably best reserved for copying a range a short distance from the original.

Moving Entries

When working with two different worksheets in the same workbook, it is sometimes easier to display each worksheet in a separate window. You can use the New Window command to display a copy of the current workbook in a second window. The workbooks are distinguished by numbers displayed in the window title bars, after their names. In the following example, we'll first display a copy of INVOICES in a second window, and then we'll move entries from the worksheet in one window to the worksheet in the other window.

1. Choose the New Window command from the Window menu. Excel displays a copy of the workbook in the new window and names the window INVOICES.XLS:2.

2. Click Window on the menu bar to drop down the menu again, and notice that the names of the two windows appear at the bottom of the menu. Click INVOICES.XLS:1 to display it.

3. To show both windows on the screen at the same time, choose Arrange from the Window menu to display this dialog box:

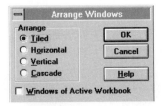

4. Click OK to accept the default Tiled option. Your window now looks like the one shown on the next page.

Other window arrangements

In addition to the Tiled option, which arranges windows like tiles on a counter, the Arrange Windows dialog box offers three other configurations. Selecting the Horizontal option allocates an equal amount of horizontal space to each open window, whereas selecting Vertical allocates an equal amount of vertical space. Selecting Cascade arranges the windows so that they overlap in a fan, with the title bar of each one visible. To arrange only the windows of the current workbook, select the Windows Of Active Workbook option.

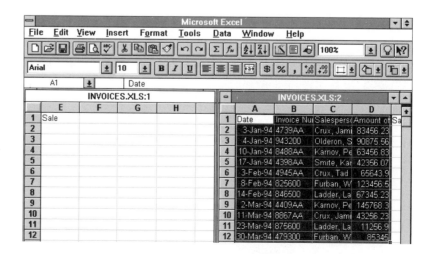

The procedure for moving cell entries is almost identical to that for copying entries. Again, you use two commands: Cut and Paste. You can choose these commands from the Edit menu, or you can click the equivalent buttons.

1. In INVOICES.XLS:1, use the bottom scroll bar to bring columns E through H into view. Then select E1:H12 and click the Cut button.

2. Activate INVOICES.XLS:2 by clicking its title bar.

3. Use the tab scrolling buttons to display Sheet3's tab, and then click the tab to display Sheet3.

4. With cell A1 in Sheet3 selected, click the Paste button. Excel instantly moves the entries from Sheet1 of INVOICES.XLS:1 to Sheet3 of INVOICES.XLS:2. Your worksheets now look like those shown here:

You can also move entries by dragging them with the mouse. Follow these steps:

1. With A1:D12 highlighted in Sheet3 of INVOICES.XLS:2, move the pointer over the right border of the selected range, where it changes to a hollow arrow.

2. Hold down the left mouse button and drag to the right until the outline of the selection is over the range E1:H12. (The worksheet scrolls to the left when you drag the pointer into the right scroll bar.)

3. Release the mouse button. Excel moves the entries in the selected cells to their new location.

   Now that you are finished moving data between sheets, you can close the second window.

1. Close the INVOICES.XLS:2 window by double-clicking its Control menu icon—the fat hyphen in the box at the left end of the window's title bar.

Closing windows

2. Now maximize the INVOICES.XLS window by clicking the Maximize button, the upward-pointing arrow at the right end of the title bar.

Inserting and Deleting Cells

It is a rare person who can create a worksheet from scratch without ever having to tinker with its design—moving this block of data, changing that heading, or adding or deleting a column here and there. In this section, we'll show you how to insert and delete cells. Follow these steps:

1. Press Ctrl+Home to move to cell A1.

Inserting columns

2. Click the column D header—the box containing the letter D—to select the entire column.

3. Right-click the column and choose Insert from the column's shortcut menu. Excel inserts an entire blank column in front of the Amount of Sale column which, as you'll see on the next page, is now column E.

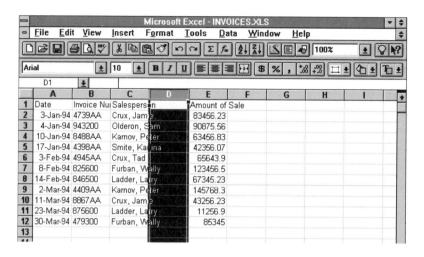

Inserting rows

Inserting a row works exactly the same way as inserting a column. You simply click the row header—the box containing the row number—to select the entire row and choose Insert from either the row's shortcut menu or the Edit menu.

What if you need to insert only a few cells and inserting an entire column or row will mess up some of your entries? You can insert cells anywhere you need them, as you'll see by following these steps:

Inserting cells

1. Select E1:E10—all but two of the cells containing entries in column E—and choose Cells from the Insert menu. Excel displays this dialog box:

Because you have selected a range rather than the entire column, Excel needs to know which cells to move to make room for the inserted cells.

2. Click OK to accept the default option of shifting cells to the right. Excel inserts a new blank cell to the left of each selected cell, as shown here:

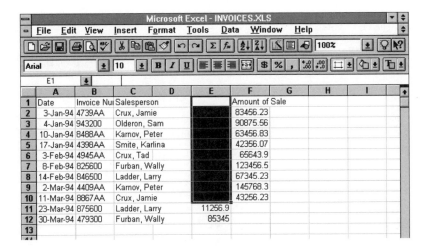

You could undo this insertion to restore the integrity of the Amount of Sale column, but instead let's delete E1:E10:

1. With E1:E10 selected, choose Delete from the Edit menu. Excel displays a Delete dialog box similar to the Insert dialog box shown on the facing page.

Deleting cells

2. Click OK to accept the default option of shifting cells to the left to fill the gap created by the deleted cells. Excel deletes the cells, and the sale amounts are now back in one column.

You can leave the empty column D where it is for now— you'll use it when we work with the INVOICES workbook again in the next chapter.

Clearing Cells

Clearing cells is different from cutting entries. Cutting entries assumes that you will paste the entries somewhere else, whereas clearing cells simply erases the entries. In the following example, you'll first clear some cells on Sheet3, and then you'll clear cells on Sheet2.

1. Click the Sheet3 tab and select E1:H12.

2. Choose Clear from the Edit menu. Excel displays the submenu shown on the next page.

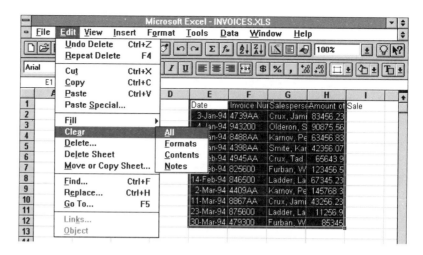

The All option clears both the formats and contents of the cell. Formats clears only the cell formats, and Contents clears only the cell contents. Notes clears any notes that you have attached to the selected cells, leaving the formats and contents intact.

3. Choose All. The entries in the range disappear.

4. Display Sheet2 and clear A1:H12 by pressing the Delete key. Excel clears the contents of the cells. (When you press Delete, Excel leaves any formats and notes intact.)

5. Return to Sheet1 by clicking the Sheet1 tab.

Formatting Basics

Excel offers a variety of formatting options that let you emphasize parts of your worksheet and display data in different ways. Here we'll look at some of the formatting options available on the Formatting toolbar. We'll also show you a quick way to adjust column widths. Later, when you have more Excel experience, you might want to explore the other formatting options available in the Format Cells dialog box.

Changing Character Styles

Just as you can use headings to make tables of data easier to read, you can use styles to distinguish different categories of information. Styles change the appearance of the characters in the worksheet. For example, you might apply the Bold style

---

Attaching notes to cells

You might want to attach a note to a cell for a variety of reasons—to explain a formula or remind yourself to check an assumption, for example. Simply select the cell, choose Note from the Insert menu, and type the note in the Text Note edit box. If you want to attach more than one note, click Add, select the next cell, and replace the text of the previous note with that of the new note. When you have finished attaching notes, click OK.

to major headings and the Bold and Italic styles to minor headings to make them stand out. Because these character styles are used so often, Excel provides buttons for them. Try this:

1. Select A1:E1, the range that contains the headings.

2. Click the Bold button. The headings are now displayed in bold.

Changing Alignment

As you know, by default Excel left-aligns text and right-aligns values. You can override the default alignment by using the Alignment buttons. Here's how:

1. With A1:E1 still selected, click each Alignment button, noting its effect.

2. When you're ready, click the Center button, which is a typical choice for headings.

Changing Column Widths

As a finishing touch for your first worksheet, you'll want to adjust the widths of columns B, C, D, and E so that the column headings fit neatly in their cells. Here's what you do:

1. Move the mouse pointer to the dividing line between the headers of columns B and C. The pointer shape changes to a vertical bar with two opposing arrows.

2. Hold down the left mouse button and drag to the right until column B is wide enough to display the Invoice Number heading. Release the mouse button when you think that the heading will fit in the cell.

3. Change the width of column E using the same method. Move the mouse pointer between the headers of columns E and F. Then hold down the mouse button and drag to the right until column E is wide enough to display its heading.

Now we'll widen columns C and D using a different method:

1. Select C1:D1 and choose Column and then Width from the Format menu. Excel displays the Column Width dialog box shown on the next page.

Column width shortcuts

To adjust the width of a column to fit its longest entry, select the column and choose Column and then AutoFit Selection from the Format menu, or double-click the column header's right border. To reset a column to the standard width, select the column, choose Column and then Standard Width from the Format menu, and then click OK. To change the standard width, choose Column and then Standard Width, type a new value in the Standard Width edit box, and click OK. (Columns whose widths you have already adjusted retain their custom widths.)

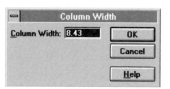

Because you have not adjusted the widths of columns C and D before, 8.43—the standard width—is displayed in the Column Width edit box.

2. Type *13* and press Enter, the keyboard equivalent of clicking OK. Here's the result:

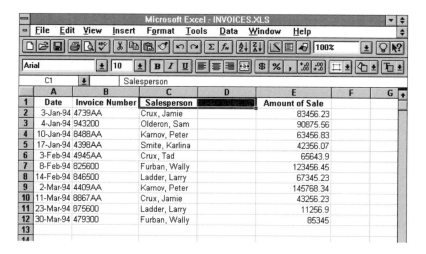

3. Click the Save button to save your changes.

Adjusting row height

You can adjust the height of rows the same way you adjust the width of columns. Simply drag the bottom header border of the row up or down, or choose Row and then Height from the Format menu to make the row shorter or taller.

Working with Multiple Workbooks

Up to now you have been working with multiple worksheets within one workbook. Excel also allows you to work with multiple workbooks at the same time. In the following examples, you'll open a new workbook, move information between workbooks, and then move a sheet from one workbook to another. Let's get going:

1. Click the New Workbook button or choose New from the File menu. Excel displays a new workbook, called Book2.

2. To see both workbooks at the same time, choose Arrange from the Window menu and click OK to accept the default Tiled option. Your screen now looks like this:

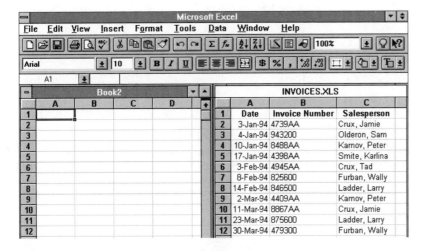

Copying Entries Between Workbooks

The procedure for copying information between workbooks is the same as for copying between sheets in one workbook. Follow these steps:

1. Activate INVOICES.XLS by clicking its title bar.

2. Select A1:E12 and click the Copy button.

3. Click cell A1 in Book2 and click the Paste button. Here is the result:

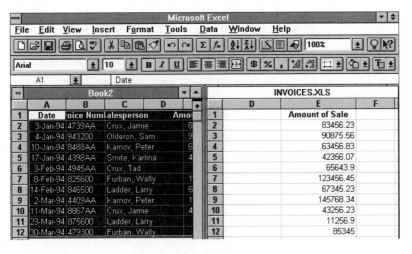

4. Press Ctrl+Home to move to cell A1.

Copying sheets

You can copy a sheet within your current workbook or to another workbook. Select the sheet you want to copy and choose Move Or Copy Sheet from the Edit menu. In the To Book edit box of the dialog box that appears, specify the destination workbook. In the Before Sheet edit box, specify the sheet that will follow the copied sheet. Then select the Create A Copy option and click OK.

Moving Sheets Between Workbooks

A sheet can easily be moved within a workbook or from one workbook to another. For this example, we'll move a worksheet from Book2 to INVOICES, but first we'll rename the tab of the worksheet we're going to move so that we can easily identify it.

Renaming sheets

1. In Book2, double-click the Sheet1 tab to display the Rename Sheet dialog box:

2. Type *Sales* in the Name edit box and press Enter. Excel displays the new name on the sheet tab.

3. Point to the Sales tab and hold down the left mouse button. The pointer is now an arrow with a sheet attached to it.

4. Drag the sheet pointer until it sits between Sheet1 and Sheet2 of the INVOICES workbook. Excel indicates with an arrowhead where it will place the Sales sheet.

5. Release the mouse button. The Sales sheet now appears in INVOICES, as shown here:

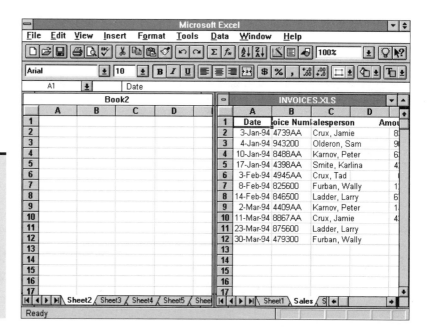

Adding sheets to a workbook

You can add a new sheet to the workbook by using the Worksheet command on the Insert menu. Excel inserts the new worksheet in front of the current sheet.

Deleting Sheets

Before deleting a sheet from a workbook, always display it. Excel permanently deletes the sheet, so it is wise to do a quick visual confirmation before sending a sheet into oblivion. In this example, we'll delete the sheet we just moved to IN-VOICES and then close Book2.

1. With the Sales sheet active, choose the Delete Sheet command from the Edit menu. Excel warns you that the sheet will be permanently deleted.

2. Click OK. Excel removes the Sales sheet from the INVOICES workbook.

3. Activate Book2 and close it by double-clicking its Control menu icon. When Excel asks whether you want to save your changes to Book2, click No.

4. Maximize the INVOICES.XLS window and click the Sheet1 tab to display its worksheet.

5. Press Ctrl+Home to clear the selection and make cell A1 the active cell.

Getting Help

This tour of Excel has covered a lot of ground in just a few pages, and you might be wondering how you will manage to retain it all. Don't worry. If you forget how to carry out a particular task, help is never far away. For example, let's see how you would remind yourself of the steps for saving a workbook:

1. Click the Help button on the Standard toolbar. The pointer becomes an arrow with a question mark attached to it. ←

2. Move the Help pointer to File on the menu bar and click to drop down the menu.

3. Click Save to display a Help window containing information about the Save command. Your screen now looks like the one shown on the next page.

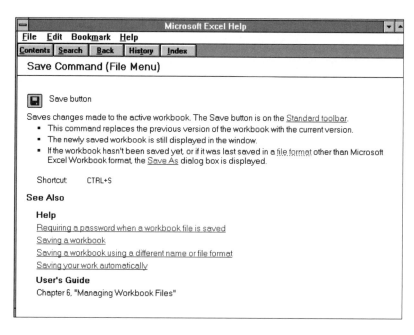

Clicking a word with a dotted underscore displays a pop-up definition, and clicking a topic with a solid underscore takes you to that topic. Clicking an item in the Help section displays a How To box with step-by-step instructions.

4. Click the Contents button below the menu bar to display the main topics of information available for Excel.

5. Click the Index button to display an alphabetical list of topics. The letters at the top of the screen provide a quick way of moving through the index.

6. Click the Search button to display this dialog box:

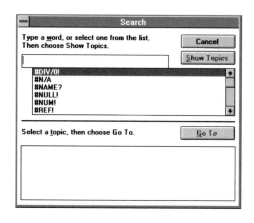

Using the TipWizard

The TipWizard monitors your actions and lets you know when it has advice to offer about your work habits by turning on the TipWizard's "light bulb" button (second from the right on the Standard toolbar). When you click the button, the TipWizard displays its tip in a toolbar below the other toolbars. The Tip Help button at the right end of the TipWizard toolbar takes you to more information about the tip. After you have read the tip, you can remove the TipWizard toolbar by clicking the TipWizard button again.

7. Enter the topic you're looking for; in this case, type *moving*. Excel scrolls its list of major topics to the first one that begins with *moving*. Click Show Topics to display a list of subtopics, select one, and click Go To to display the requested information.

8. Explore the other aspects of Excel's Help system, and then click the Back button to retrace your steps.

9. When you're ready, choose Exit from the File menu to close the Help window and return to your worksheet.

Quitting Excel

Well, that's it for the basic tour. All that's left is to show you how to end an Excel session. Follow these steps:

1. Choose Exit from the File menu.

2. When Excel asks if you want to save the changes you have made to the open worksheet, click Yes.

2

Analyzing Information

What you will learn...

Set custom headers
and footers

Preliminary Sales Analysis
1st Quarter, 1994

Dress up headings by varying the font and size

Total Sales	$	822,216.74
Average Sales		$74,746.98
Highest Sale		$145,768.34
Lowest Sale		$11,256.90
Commission		5%
Sales Expense		$41,110.84

Set up a calculation area for your formulas

Invoice Details

Type one character and repeat it in a range

Date	Quarter	Invoice Number	Salesperson	Office	Amount of Sale
1/3/94	1	4739AA	Crux, Jamie	East	$83,456.23
1/4/94	1	943200	Olderon, Sam	West	$90,875.56
1/10/94	1	8488AA	Karnov, Peter	East	$63,456.83
1/17/94	1	4398AA	Smite, Karlina	East	$42,356.07
2/3/94	1	4945AA	Crux, Tad	East	$65,643.90
2/8/94	1	825600	Furban, Wally	West	$123,456.45
2/14/94	1	846500	Ladder, Larry	West	$67,345.23
3/2/94	1	4409AA	Karnov, Peter	East	$145,768.34
3/11/94	1	8867AA	Crux, Jamie	East	$43,256.23
3/23/94	1	875600	Ladder, Larry	West	$11,256.90
3/30/94	1	479300	Furban, Wally	West	$85,345.00
					$822,216.74

Set up a calcu-
lation area for
your formulas

Turn off grid
lines so that
data stands out

Total a column of
values with the
click of a button

Use an IF function to
assign dates to quarters

Use a currency format
to display values as
dollars and cents

Chapter 1 covered some Excel basics, and you now know enough to create simple tables. But you are missing the essential piece of information that turns a table into a worksheet: how to enter formulas. The whole purpose of building worksheets is to have Excel perform calculations for you. In this chapter, we show you how to retrieve the INVOICES workbook and enter formulas to analyze sales. (If you don't work in sales, you can adapt the worksheet to analyze other sources of income such as service fees or subscriptions.) Along the way, we cover some powerful techniques for manipulating data and a few principles of worksheet design. Finally, we spell check and print Sheet1 of the INVOICES workbook. So fire up Excel and then we'll get started.

Opening Existing Workbooks

When you first start Excel, the workbook window contains a blank document named Book1. You can open a workbook you have already created using several methods. If the workbook is one of the last four you have worked with, you can simply choose the file from the bottom of the File menu. Otherwise, you can use the Open button on the Standard toolbar or the Open command on the File menu to retrieve the workbook. We'll use the first method:

1. Choose INVOICES.XLS from the bottom of the File menu. Excel displays the table you created in Chapter 1.

Simple Calculations

Excel has many powerful functions that are a sort of shorthand for the various formulas used in mathematical, logical, statistical, financial, trigonometric, logarithmic, and other types of calculations. However, the majority of worksheets created with Excel involve simple arithmetic. In this section, we show you how to use four arithmetic operators (+, −, *, and /) to add, subtract, multiply, and divide, and then we introduce two Excel features with which you can quickly add sets of numeric values.

Doing Arithmetic

In Excel you begin a formula with an equal sign (=). In the simplest formulas, the equal sign is followed by a set of values separated by +, –, *, or /, such as

=5+3+2

If you enter this formula in any blank cell in your worksheet, Excel displays the result 10.

Let's experiment with a few formulas. We'll start by inserting a couple of blank rows:

1. Click the header for row 1 and drag down through the header for row 2 to select the two rows.

Inserting multiple rows

2. Right-click anywhere in the selected rows and choose Insert from the shortcut menu. Because you selected two rows, Excel inserts two blank rows above the table, moving the table down so that it begins in row 3.

Now we're ready to construct a formula in cell A1, using some of the values in the Amount of Sale column. You tell Excel to use a value simply by clicking the cell that contains it. Follow these steps:

1. Click cell A1 and type an equal sign followed by an opening parenthesis.

2. Click cell E4. Excel inserts the cell reference E4 in the cell and the formula bar.

Entering cell references in formulas

3. Type a plus sign and click cell E5. Excel adds the cell reference E5 to the formula.

4. Continue to build the formula by typing plus signs and clicking cells E6, E7, and E8.

5. Type a closing parenthesis followed by a / (the division operator), and then type 5. The formula now looks like the one on the next page.

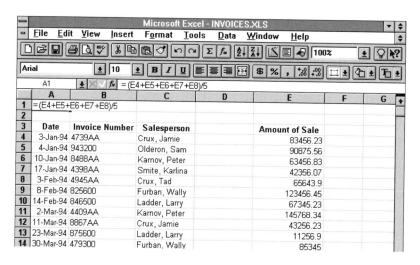

This formula tells Excel to first add the amounts in cells E4, E5, E6, E7, and E8 and then divide the result by 5, to obtain the average of the five amounts.

6. Click the Confirm button. Excel displays the result of the formula, 69157.72, in cell A1.

You can use this technique to create any simple formula. Start by typing an equal sign, then enter a value or click the cell that contains the value, type the appropriate arithmetic operator, enter the next value, and so on. Unless you tell Excel to do otherwise, the program performs multiplication and division before addition and subtraction. If you need parts of the formula to be carried out in a different order, use parentheses as we did in this example to override the default order.

Order of precedence →

Totaling Columns of Values

Although this method of creating a formula is simple enough, it would be tedious to have to type and click to add a long series of values. Fortunately, Excel automates the addition process with a very useful button: the AutoSum button.

Using the AutoSum Button

The AutoSum button will probably become one of your most often-used Excel buttons. In fact, using this button is so easy that we'll dispense with explanations and simply show you what to do:

1. Click cell E15.

Displaying formulas

By default, Excel displays the results of formulas in cells, not their underlying formulas. To see the actual underlying formulas in the worksheet, choose Options from the Tools menu, display the View options, select Formulas in the Window Options section, and click OK. Excel widens the cells so that you can see the formulas. Simply deselect the Formulas option to redisplay the results.

2. Click the AutoSum button on the Standard toolbar. Excel looks first above and then to the left of the active cell for an adjacent range of values to total. Excel assumes that you want to total the values above E15 and enters the SUM function in cell E15 and in the formula bar. Your worksheet looks like this:

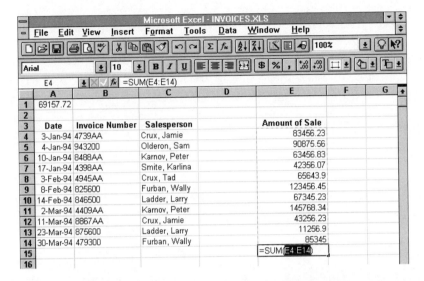

3. Click the Confirm button to enter the formula in cell E15. Excel displays the result 822216.74—the sum of the values in E4:E14.

That was easy. The AutoSum button will serve you well whenever you want a total to appear at the bottom of a column or to the right of a row of values. But what if you want the total to appear elsewhere on the worksheet? Knowing how to create SUM functions from scratch gives you more flexibility.

Using the SUM Function

Let's go back and dissect the SUM function that Excel inserted in cell E15 when you clicked the AutoSum button, so that you can examine the function's components.

With cell E15 selected, you can see the following entry in the formula bar:

=SUM(E4:E14)

Like all formulas, the SUM function begins with an equal sign (=). Next comes the function name in capital letters, followed by a set of parentheses enclosing the reference to the range

Arguments →

containing the amounts you want to total. This reference is the SUM function's *argument*. An argument answers questions such as "What?" or "How?" and gives Excel the additional information it needs to perform the function. In the case of SUM, Excel needs only one piece of information—the references of the cells you want to total. As you'll see later, Excel might need several pieces of information to carry out other functions, and you enter an argument for each piece.

Creating a SUM function from scratch is not particularly difficult. For practice, follow these steps:

1. Press Ctrl+Home to move to cell A1, and type this:

   =SUM(

   When you begin typing, the cell's old value is overwritten.

2. Select E4:E14 on the worksheet in the usual way. Excel inserts the reference E4:E14 after the opening parenthesis.

3. Type a closing parenthesis and press Enter. Excel displays in cell A1 the total of the values in the Amount of Sale column—822216.7. Because the widths of cells A1 and E15 are different, their displayed results are slightly different, but their underlying values are identical.

Referencing Formula Cells in Other Formulas

After you create a formula in one cell, you can use its result in other formulas simply by referencing its cell. To see how this works, follow these steps:

1. Select cell B1 and type an equal sign.

2. Click cell A1, which contains the SUM function you just entered, type a / (the division operator), and then type *11*.

3. Click the Confirm button. Excel displays the result—the average of the invoice amounts—in cell B1. (We discuss an easier way to calculate averages on page 51.)

4. Press the Delete key to erase both the experimental formula and its result from cell B1.

Function names

When you type a function name, such as SUM, in the formula bar, you don't have to type it in capital letters. Excel capitalizes the function name for you when you complete the entry. If Excel does not respond in this way, you have probably entered the function name incorrectly.

Naming Cells and Ranges

Many of the calculations that you might want to perform on this worksheet—for example, calculating each invoice amount as a percentage of total sales—will use the total you have calculated in cell A1. You could include a copy of the SUM function now in cell A1 in these other calculations, or you could simply reference cell A1. The latter method seems quick and simple, but what if you subsequently move the formula in A1 to another location? Excel gives you a way to reference this formula no matter where on the worksheet you move it. You can assign cell A1 a name and then use the name in any calculations that involve the total.

You assign a name to a cell by using the Name command on the Insert menu. Follow these steps:

1. Select cell A1 and choose Name and then Define from the Insert menu. Excel displays the Define Name dialog box:

Assigning cell names

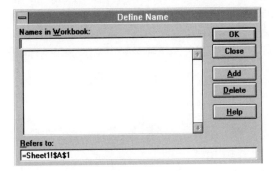

The reference Sheet1!$A$1 is displayed in the Refers To edit box. This absolute reference points to cell A1 on Sheet1 of the current workbook. (For an explanation of absolute references, see page 58.)

2. Type *Total* in the Names In Workbook edit box.

3. Click OK to assign the name Total to cell A1. If you look at the name box to the left of the formula bar, you'll see that Excel now refers to the cell by the name you just entered, instead of by the cell reference A1. You can use either designation in formulas.

> **Name conventions**
>
> Certain rules apply when you name cells or ranges. Although you can use a number within the name, you must start the name with a letter, an underscore, or a backslash. Spaces are not allowed within the name, so you should use underscore characters to represent spaces. For example, you cannot use 1992 as a name, but you can use Totals_1992.

To see how Excel uses the names you assign, try this:

Using cell names

1. Click cell E15, which currently contains the SUM function you inserted earlier in the chapter.

2. Type =*Total* and press Enter. The worksheet does not appear to change, but now instead of two SUM functions, the worksheet contains only one. You have told Excel to assign the value of the cell named Total, which contains the SUM function, to cell E15.

You can also assign names to ranges. Let's assign the name Amount to the cells containing amounts in column E:

Assigning range names

1. Select E4:E14 and choose Name and then Define from the Insert menu.

2. Type *Amount* in the Names In Workbook edit box and then click OK.

Now let's replace the range reference in the SUM function in cell A1 with the new range name:

1. Click A1 to select it and display its contents in the formula bar.

2. Drag through the E4:E14 reference in the formula bar to highlight it.

Selecting a name from the name list

3. Click the down arrow to the right of the name box to display the list of names assigned in this workbook:

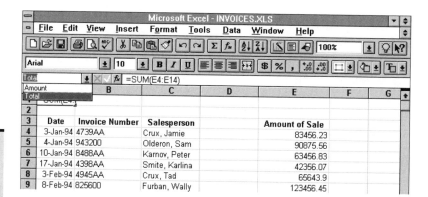

Jumping to named cells

To move quickly to a named cell, press the F5 key. When Excel displays the Go To dialog box, select the name of the cell you want to move to, and click OK.

4. Click Amount. Excel replaces the range reference with the name assigned to the range, and the formula bar now reads =*SUM(Amount)*.

5. Click the Confirm button. The total in cell A1 remains the same as before, even though you've changed the formula.

6. Click the Save button to save your work.

From now on, we won't give you specific instructions to save your work, but you should get in the habit of saving often, perhaps after working through each example.

Efficient Data Display

Before we discuss other calculations you might want to perform with this worksheet, let's look at ways to format your information to make it easier to read. We'll show you how to make the results of your calculations stand out from your data and how to format the data itself so that it is neat and consistent. As your worksheets grow in complexity, you'll find that paying attention to such details will keep you oriented and help others understand your results.

Creating a Calculation Area

Usually when you create a worksheet, you are interested not so much in the individual pieces of information as in the results of the calculations you perform on the pieces. The current worksheet fits neatly on one screen, but often worksheets of this type include several screenfuls of information. It's a good idea to design your worksheets so that the important information is easily accessible and in a predictable location. For these reasons, we leave room in the top left corner of our worksheets for a calculation area. This habit is useful for the following reasons:

- We don't have to scroll around looking for totals and other results.

Advantages

- We can print just the first page of a worksheet to get a report of the most pertinent information.

- We can easily jump to the calculation area from anywhere on the worksheet by pressing Ctrl+Home to move to cell A1.

Let's create an area at the top of Sheet1 of the INVOICES workbook for a title and a set of calculations. We'll start by freeing up some space at the top of the worksheet:

Moving a range

1. Select A1:E15 and use the Cut and Paste buttons to move the selection to A10:E24.

2. Press Ctrl+Home. Your screen now looks like this:

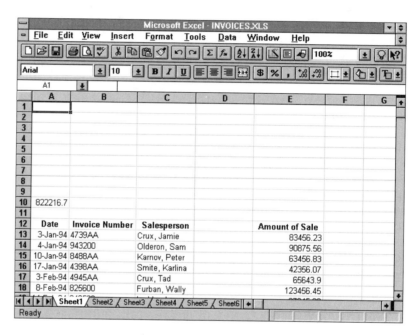

Flexible repeating characters

You can use any character or group of characters to fill a cell or range of cells. Some common examples of repeating characters are hyphens and equal signs. You might want to experiment with combinations, such as asterisk-hyphen-space, to create different effects. Using the Fill option as described here is more efficient than typing countless characters, not only because it saves typing time but also because the Fill option responds to changes you make to column widths. For example, if you decrease the width of column A, Excel adjusts the number of asterisks so that they continue to fill the selected ranges.

Now let's enter a title for the worksheet:

1. In cell A1, type *Preliminary Sales Analysis* and press the Down Arrow key.

2. In cell A2, type *1st Quarter, 1994* and press Enter.

Next, we'll set off the calculation area. With Excel, you can get really fancy, using borders and shading to draw attention to calculation results. Later in this chapter, we show you some special techniques for formatting your worksheets. For now, though, let's draw lines of asterisks above and below the area, using one of Excel's special alignment formats:

1. With cell A3 selected, type one asterisk and click the Confirm button.

2. Now select A3:E3 and choose the Cells command from the Format menu. In the Format Cells dialog box, click the Alignment tab to display these options:

Repeating a pattern

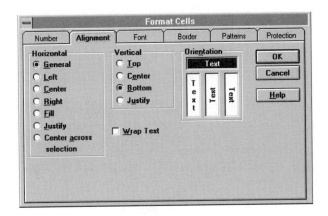

3. In the Horizontal section, select Fill and click OK.

4. Hold down the Ctrl key, point to the bottom border of the selected range, and drag a copy of the row of asterisks down to A9:E9.

Now that we have created a calculation area, let's move the calculation in cell A10. Follow these steps:

1. Select cell A4, type *Total Sales*, and press Enter.

Moving formulas

2. Select cell A10 and use the Cut and Paste buttons to move the formula to cell B4. Here are the results:

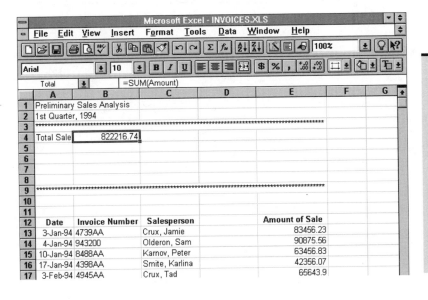

Moving formulas

When you move the formula from cell A1 to cell A10, the formula remains correct. How can you move a formula without disturbing the results? The reference in the formula is relative, meaning that it identifies cells according to their location relative to the formula cell. See page 58 for more information.

Formatting Text

In Chapter 1, you learned how to format text in simple ways—using buttons on the toolbar to change alignment and make text bold. In this section, we'll get a bit more elaborate. First let's make the worksheet's title larger so that it really stands out:

Changing fonts and sizes

1. Select cell A1 and choose Cells from the Format menu.

2. In the Format Cells dialog box, click the Font tab to display these options:

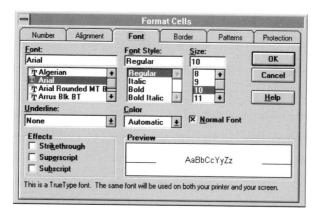

3. Click Bold in the Font Style section, select 22 from the Size list, and then click OK. Notice that the height of row 1 increases to accommodate the larger font.

4. Right-click cell A2 and then choose Format Cells from the shortcut menu.

5. In the Format Cells dialog box, click Bold Italic in the Font Style section, select 14 from the Size list, and click OK.

Now let's center the titles above the calculation area:

Centering across columns

1. Select A1:E2 and click the Center Across Columns button on the Formatting toolbar. Excel centers the titles over the selected area, but the titles are still stored in cells A1 and A2.

Now let's add another touch:

1. Select A4:A8, and click the Bold button on the Formatting toolbar.

Why did we tell you to select the empty cells below Total Sales before applying the Bold style? Try this:

1. Select cell A5, type *Average Sales*, and click the Confirm button. The new heading is bold because you already applied the Bold style to cell A5.

2. Choose Column and then AutoFit Selection from the Format menu to widen column A so that the headings fit within the column. From now on, adjust the column width as necessary to see your work.

Fitting columns to entries

3. Press Ctrl+Home. Here's the result of your formatting:

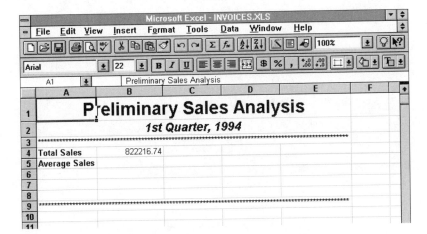

Displaying Dollars and Cents

With the exception of the date values in column A, Excel has displayed the values you've entered so far in its default General format. With this format, Excel simply displays what you typed (or what it thinks you typed). For example, when you entered the dates in Chapter 1, Excel displayed them in a date format.

Excel provides several formats that you can use to change the way the values look. Try this:

1. Right-click cell E13 and choose Format Cells from the shortcut menu.

2. In the Format Cells dialog box, click the Number tab to display the options shown on the next page.

Entering in format

By default, Excel formats values the way you enter them. For example, entering $123,456.78 applies the Currency format to the current cell. Entering 12-Dec-94 applies the d-mmm-yy date format to the current cell.

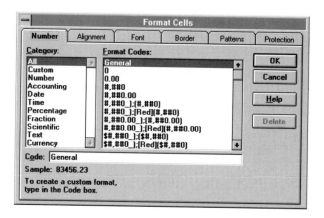

In the Category list, Excel highlights All, and in the Format Codes list, Excel highlights General—the default settings. In the bottom left corner, a Sample area shows you how the value in E13 looks with the selected format. Here are the formats you'll probably use most frequently:

Format	Effect
Currency formats	Add a dollar sign in front of the value, use commas to group the digits by threes, and display two decimal places (cents)
#,##0 format	Inserts commas to group the digits in values greater than 999 by threes, and displays two decimal places
Percentage formats	Display the value as a percentage and append a percent sign

For expediency, three of these formats have corresponding buttons on the Formatting toolbar.

3. Select Currency from the Category list and the third currency option from the Format Codes list, which displays numbers with a dollar sign and two decimal places.

4. Click OK.

You can save time by applying number formats using the buttons on the Formatting toolbar. Here's how:

1. Select B4:B8 and click the Currency Style button. Excel formats the selected cells with a dollar sign and two decimal places, as shown here:

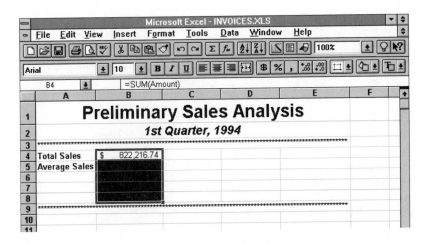

2. To see the Currency format for negative values, select cell B5, type *–1234*, and press Enter. Here's the result:

Negative dollar amounts

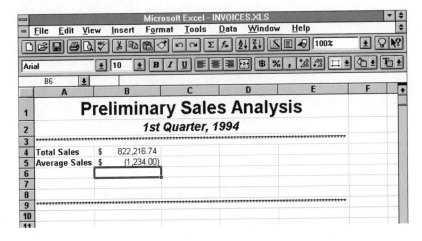

As you can see, Excel displays the negative value in parentheses, aligning the value with the positive value above it and adding a dollar sign, a comma to separate hundreds from thousands, and two zeros to the right of the decimal point.

Formatting Decimal Places

You can change the number of decimal places simply by using the Increase Decimal and Decrease Decimal buttons, as follows:

1. Select B4:B5 and click the Decrease Decimal button twice. Excel rounds the values in the selected cells to whole dollars.

2. With B4:B5 still highlighted, click the Increase Decimal button twice to restore the two decimal places.

Formatting Dates

In Chapter 1, we entered dates in column A in a variety of formats. Now we'll show you how to change the date format to reflect the needs of your worksheet. Let's experiment with the dates you entered earlier in column A:

1. Select A13:A23, right-click the selection, and choose Format Cells from the shortcut menu. Excel displays the Number tab options with the cells' current format highlighted.

2. Select the d-mmm format and click OK.

3. Return to the Format Cells dialog box and experiment with the other date formats. Click the different options in the Format Codes list and view the effect in the Sample area.

4. Select the m/d/yy format and click OK.

Copying Styles and Formats

In Excel, you can save a lot of formatting time by copying combinations of styles and formats from one cell to other cells. For example, if you format your headings to be bold and centered, you can apply those styles to any cells in the worksheet simply by copying them. Let's give it a try:

1. Select cell A10, type *Invoice Details*, and press Enter.

2. Select cell A12, which contains a heading that is bold and centered, and click the Format Painter button on the Standard toolbar.

3. Move the pointer, which now has the shape of a plus sign with a paintbrush, to cell A10 and click. Excel immediately applies both the bold and centered styles to the selected cell.

Now let's format the remaining values in the Amount of Sale column as currency, this time copying the format from cell E13:

1. Select cell E13 and click the Format Painter button.

2. Select E14:E24. When you release the mouse button, Excel applies the Currency format from cell E13 to the selected

Underlying vs. displayed

After you apply a format, the value displayed in the cell might look different from the value in the formula bar. For example, 345.6789 is displayed in its cell as $345.68 after you apply the Currency format. When performing calculations, Excel uses the value in the formula bar, not the displayed value.

range, adding dollar signs, commas, and two decimal places to the values. Your worksheet now looks like this:

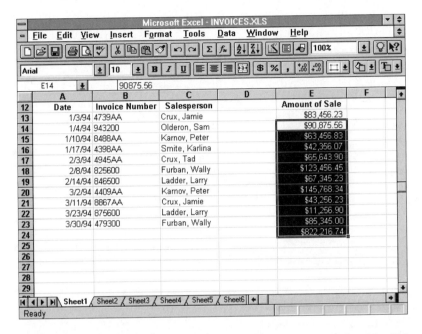

From this simple example, you can see how easy it is to build complex combinations of formatting that you can apply with a couple of clicks of the mouse button.

More Calculations

Now let's return to the calculation area and perform some more calculations on the sales data, starting with the average sales.

Averaging Values

To find the average amount for the invoices we've entered in this worksheet, we'll use Excel's AVERAGE function. We'll use the Function Wizard button on the Standard toolbar to avoid making errors while typing function names, and to make sure we include all the arguments Excel needs to calculate the function. The Function Wizard walks you through the steps of building the formula.

1. Select cell B5 and click the Function Wizard button. Excel displays the first Function Wizard dialog box shown on the next page, which lists the most frequently used functions.

The Function Wizard

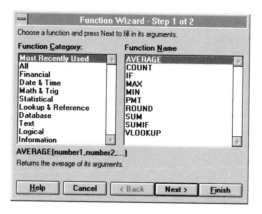

2. Since AVERAGE is already highlighted, click the Next button to display the second dialog box:

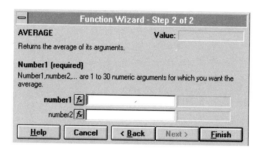

The dialog box contains a definition of the function and its arguments. The insertion point sits in the Number1 edit box, waiting for you to enter a number, cell reference, name, formula, or another function.

3. Move the dialog box and select E13:E23 in the worksheet. The formula now includes the reference of the selection:

Moving dialog boxes

To enter a cell or range reference in an edit box, you can click the cell or select the range on the worksheet. If the dialog box obscures the desired cell or range, simply move the dialog box out of the way by pointing to its title bar, holding down the mouse button, and dragging until you can see the part of the worksheet you're interested in.

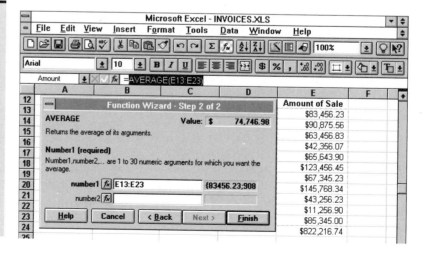

4. Click the Finish button to enter the formula in cell B5, and press Ctrl+Home to see the results. Excel displays $74,746.98 in cell B5.

Identifying Highest and Lowest Sales

Excel provides two functions that instantly identify the highest and lowest values in a group. To understand the benefits of these functions, imagine that the INVOICES worksheet contains data from not 11 but 111 invoices! Let's start with the highest sale:

1. Select cell A6, type *Highest Sale*, and press the Right Arrow key to confirm the entry and select cell B6.

2. Click the Function Wizard button and select MAX from the Function Name list. This function gives the maximum value from the range we select.

3. Click the Next button to display the second dialog box.

4. Select E13:E23, click Finish, and press Ctrl+Home. Excel enters the highest sale amount, $145,768.34, in cell B6.

Now for the formula for the lowest sale, which we'll type from scratch:

1. Select cell A7, type *Lowest Sale*, and press Right Arrow.

2. Type *=MIN(E13:E23)* and press Enter. Excel displays the result, $11,256.90, in cell B7.

Calculating with Names

The last calculation we'll make with this set of data involves the Total Sales value from cell B4. As a gross indicator of sales expenses, let's calculate the total sales commission:

1. First insert a couple of new rows in the calculation area by dragging through the headers for rows 8 and 9, right-clicking the selection, and choosing Insert from the shortcut menu.

2. In cell A8, type *Commission* and press Right Arrow.

3. Type *6%* and click the Confirm button.

A function for every task

Excel has over 300 functions. Many functions are provided for common business and financial tasks—some of them quite complex. To get more information about a function, choose Contents from the Help menu and then select Reference Information. From the list displayed, choose Worksheet Functions. Excel displays a list of function information. Select Alphabetical List Of Worksheet Functions to see a list of the functions with brief descriptions of each one.

4. With cell B8 still active, choose Name and then Define from the Insert menu. Excel scans the adjacent cells and suggests the name Commission. Click OK.

Now for the formula that will calculate the commission:

1. Select cell A9, type *Sales Expense*, and press Right Arrow.

2. With cell B9 selected, type the formula =*total*commission* and press Enter. Excel multiplies the value in the cell named Total (B4) by the value in the cell named Commission (B8) and displays the result, $49,333.00, in cell B9. (Notice that Excel displays the result of the formula in the Currency format. When you inserted two rows earlier, those rows assumed the formatting of the selected rows.)

Changing the value of a named cell →

3. Now select cell B8, type *5%*, and click the Confirm button. Instantly, the value in cell B9 changes to reflect the new commission rate, as shown here:

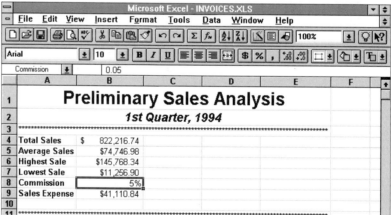

Text values as arguments

When entering text values as arguments in a formula, you must enclose them in quotation marks. Otherwise, Excel thinks the text is a name and displays the error value #NAME? in the cell. For example,

=RIGHT("Excel",2)

gives the value "el," but

=RIGHT(Excel,2)

results in an error—unless the range name Excel happens to be assigned to a cell or range on the worksheet.

If a hundred calculations throughout the worksheet referenced the cell named Commission, Excel would adjust all their results to reflect this one change. Powerful stuff!

Formulas That Make Decisions

There will be times when you want Excel to carry out one task under certain circumstances and another task if those circumstances don't apply. To give this kind of instruction to Excel, you use the IF function.

Using the IF Function

In its simplest form, the IF function tests the value of a cell and does one thing if the test is positive (true) and another if the test is negative (false). It requires three arguments: the test, the action to perform if the test is true, and the action to perform if the test is false. You supply the arguments one after the other within the function's parentheses, separating them with commas (no spaces). Try this:

How the IF function works

1. Select cell D4, type the following, and then press Enter:

=IF(B4=0,"TRUE","FALSE")

Excel checks whether the value in cell B4 is zero (the test), and because it isn't zero, it ignores TRUE (the action to perform if the test is true) and displays FALSE (the action to perform if the test is false) in cell D4.

2. Double-click cell D4, drag through =0 to highlight it, type *<1000000*, and press Enter. The entry in cell D4 instantly changes from FALSE to TRUE, because the value in cell B4 is less than 1 million; that is, the test is true.

In this example, the test Excel performed was a simple evaluation of the value in a cell. However, you can also build tests that involve other functions. Recall that the last two characters of the invoice numbers in column B of the worksheet indicate whether the sale originated in your company's East or West office. Suppose you want to assign East and West entries to each invoice so that you can compare the performances of the two offices. Follow these steps:

1. Select cell D14, type *Office*, and press Down Arrow.

2. In cell D15, type the following and click the Confirm button:

=IF(RIGHT(B15,2)="AA","East","West")

You have told Excel to look at the two characters at the right end of the value in cell B15 and if they are AA, to enter East in cell D15. If they are not AA, Excel is to enter West. The result is shown on the next page.

Logical operators

Here is a list of operators you can use with the IF function:

= < > <> >= <=

You can also use AND and OR to combine two or more tests. The function

=IF(AND(B4=0,B5>0),"Yes","No")

displays Yes only if both tests are true. The function

=IF(OR(B4=0,B5>0),"Yes","No")

displays Yes if either test is true.

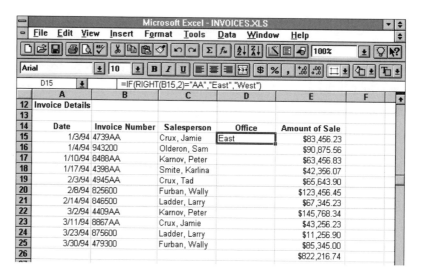

Using Nested IF Functions

When constructing conditions, you can use IF functions within IF functions. Called *nested functions*, these formulas add another dimension to the complexity of the decisions Excel can make. Here's a quick demonstration:

1. Insert a new column between columns A and B, and enter the column heading *Quarter* in cell B14.

2. Select B15:B25, right-click the selection, and choose Format Cells from the shortcut menu.

3. Select All from the Category list and General from the Format Codes list, and click OK.

4. Now select cell B15 and type this formula all on one line:

Functions within functions →

=IF(MONTH(A15)<4,1,IF(MONTH(A15)<7,2,
    IF(MONTH(A15)<10,3,4)))

5. Check your typing, paying special attention to all the parentheses, and then click the Confirm button.

You have told Excel to check the month component of the date in cell A15. If it is less than 4, Excel is to display 1 in the corresponding cell in the Quarter column. If the month is not less than 4 but is less than 7, Excel is to display 2 in the Quarter column. If it is not less than 7 but is less than 10, Excel is to display 3. Otherwise, Excel is to display 4. If you have typed the formula correctly, Excel enters 1 in cell B15.

Copying Formulas

The IF functions you just entered are arduous to type, even for good typists. Fortunately, you don't have to enter them more than once. By using AutoFill, you can copy the formula into the cells below, like this:

1. Select B15 and position the pointer over the bottom right corner of the cell. The pointer changes to the black fill handle.

2. Hold down the mouse button and drag down to cell B25. Excel copies the formula from B15 into the highlighted cells.

3. Select cell E15, and again position the pointer over the bottom right corner of the cell.

4. Hold down the mouse button and drag down to cell E25. The worksheet now looks like the one shown here:

	A	B	C	D	E	F
12	Invoice Details					
13						
14	Date	Quarter	Invoice Number	Salesperson	Office	Amount of Sal
15	1/3/94	1	4739AA	Crux, Jamie	East	$83,456.2
16	1/4/94	1	943200	Olderon, Sam	West	$90,875.5
17	1/10/94	1	8488AA	Karnov, Peter	East	$63,456.8
18	1/17/94	1	4398AA	Smite, Karlina	East	$42,356.0
19	2/3/94	1	4945AA	Crux, Tad	East	$65,643.9
20	2/8/94	1	825600	Furban, Wally	West	$123,456.4
21	2/14/94	1	846500	Ladder, Larry	West	$67,345.2
22	3/2/94	1	4409AA	Karnov, Peter	East	$145,768.3
23	3/11/94	1	8867AA	Crux, Jamie	East	$43,256.2
24	3/23/94	1	875600	Ladder, Larry	West	$11,256.9
25	3/30/94	1	479300	Furban, Wally	West	$85,345.0
26						$822,216.7

E15 = IF(RIGHT(C15,2)="AA","East","West")

5. Select cell E15 and look at the formula in the formula bar. Excel has changed the original formula

=IF(RIGHT(B15,2)="AA","East","West")

to

=IF(RIGHT(C15,2)="AA","East","West")

Duplicating a formula in multiple cells

The Fill command

You can use the Fill command to copy entries into a range of adjacent cells. Select the cell whose contents and formats you want to copy, drag through the adjacent range, and choose Fill from the Edit menu. How Excel copies the cell is determined by the command you choose from the Fill submenu. Choosing Down copies the entry down a range; choosing Right copies the entry to the right; and so on. Three related commands are also available on this submenu: Across Worksheets copies entries to the equivalent cells on a group of selected worksheets; Series fills the selection with a series of values or dates (see page 67 for more information); and Justify distributes the contents of the active cell evenly in the cells of the selected range.

Excel changed the reference to account for the addition of the Quarter column. If you click cell E16, you'll see that when you used AutoFill, Excel changed the reference so that it refers to cell C16 as its argument, not C15.

By default, Excel uses *relative references* in its formulas. Relative references refer to cells by their position in relation to the cell containing the formula. So when you copied the formula in cell E15 to cell E16, Excel changed the reference from C15 to C16—the cell in the same row and two columns to the left of the cell containing the formula. If you were to copy the formula in cell E15 to F15, Excel would change the reference from C15 to D15 so that the formula would continue to reference the cell in the same relative position.

When you don't want a reference to be copied as a relative reference, as it was in these examples, you need to use an *absolute reference*. Absolute references refer to cells by their fixed position in the worksheet. To make a reference absolute, you add dollar signs before its column letter and row number. For example, to change the reference C4:C9 to an absolute reference, you would enter it as $C$4:$C$9. You could then copy a formula that contained this reference anywhere on the worksheet and it would always refer to the range C4:C9.

References can also be partially relative and partially absolute. For example, $C3 has an absolute column reference and a relative row reference, and C$3 has a relative column reference and an absolute row reference.

Checking Spelling

Checking a selection

If you don't want to spell check an entire worksheet, select the cells you want to check and then click the Spelling button or choose Spelling from the Tools menu. (If you want to check just one cell, double-click the cell.) Excel checks only the selection.

In a moment, we'll print Sheet1 of the INVOICES workbook, but because you will usually want to spell check your worksheets before you print them, we'll pause here to discuss Excel's spell checker. You can check all or part of your worksheets for misspelled words and duplicate words within a block. From the Spelling dialog box, you can edit the dictionary Excel uses to check your work, and you can add words to or delete words from it. In this section, we'll introduce a deliberate misspelling into the INVOICES worksheet and then run a spell check to see how the spell checker works.

1. Double-click cell A9 to edit its entry directly within the cell. Delete the *e* from the end of *Expense* and press Enter. Then press Ctrl+Home to move to A1.

2. Click the Spelling button.

3. Excel starts checking the INVOICES worksheet, finds the misspelled word, and displays this dialog box:

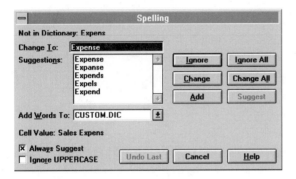

4. Excel suggests possible replacements for the misspelled word in the Suggestions list box and highlights the most likely candidate, Expense, in the Change To edit box. Click the Change button. The spell checker replaces the suspected word and continues checking the document.

5. Complete the spell check, clicking the Ignore or Ignore All buttons for all the other words that Excel stumbles over.

6. When the spell checker finishes checking the worksheet, it displays a message box. Click OK to return to the worksheet.

Printing Worksheets

If your primary purpose in learning Excel is to be able to manipulate your own information and come up with results that will guide your decision-making, your worksheets might never need to leave your computer. If, on the other hand, you want to sway the decisions of your colleagues or you need to prepare reports for your board of directors, you will probably need printed copies of your worksheets. Now is a good time to discuss how to print an Excel document.

Printer setup

If your computer can access more than one printer or if you need to set up the printer to print with Excel, click the Printer Setup button in the Print dialog box and select the printer from the Printer list. Then make any necessary adjustments, such as switching between portrait and landscape printing, by clicking the Setup button to access the printer's setup dialog box. Note that changes you make in these dialog boxes may also affect printing in other Windows applications.

Previewing Worksheets

Usually, you'll want to preview your worksheets before you print them to make sure that single-page documents fit neatly on the page and that multipage documents break in logical places. You can click the Print Preview button or choose the Print Preview command from the File menu to get a bird's-eye view of your document. Follow these steps:

1. Click the Print Preview button on the Standard toolbar. The Print Preview window opens, with a miniature version of the printed worksheet displayed, as shown here:

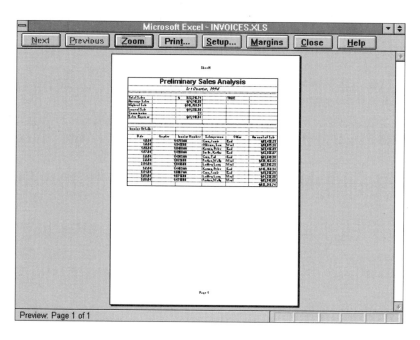

2. Move the mouse pointer over the page. The pointer changes to a small magnifying glass.

Zooming in and out

3. To examine part of the page in more detail, move the magnifying glass over that part, and click the mouse button. Excel zooms in on that portion of the page. Click again to zoom out.

Setting Up the Pages

By default, Excel prints your worksheet with gridlines around each cell, the workbook's filename as a header at the top of the page, and the page number as a footer at the bottom of the page. For presentation purposes, these default settings don't produce a very attractive printout, so you'll probably want to change them. You make these changes in the Page Setup dialog box, which Excel displays when you choose Page Setup from the File menu. When you are in Print Preview, you can also access this dialog box directly, like this:

1. Click the Setup button at the top of the Print Preview window to display a Page Setup dialog box something like this one:

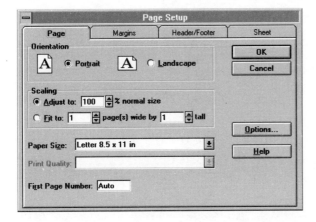

Your dialog box might differ slightly, depending on the type of printer you have. If the Page options are not displayed, click the Page tab.

2. Click the Header/Footer tab to display the Header/Footer options. You use the Custom Header and Custom Footer buttons to move to another dialog box where you can add, delete, and edit headers and footers.

3. Click Custom Header to display the Header dialog box:

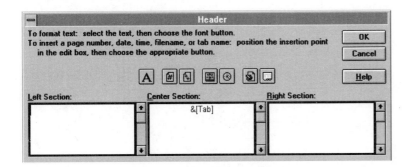

To add a header, you enter text and codes in the appropriate boxes and click the buttons in the middle of the dialog box.

Header and footer codes

The buttons in the Header and Footer dialog boxes add codes that do the following:

&[Page]	Adds current page number
&[Pages]	Inserts total number of pages
&[Date]	Adds current date
&[Time]	Adds current time
&[File]	Adds filename
&[Tab]	Adds sheet name

Here are some formatting codes:

&B	Prints following characters in bold
&I	Italicizes following characters
&U	Underlines following characters

You can also format headers and footers by selecting the text you want to format and clicking the font button (the capital A).

4. Double-click &[Tab] in the Center Section box, and type *&bInvoice Log*. The &b code tells Excel to print the text in bold.

5. Click OK to return to the Header/Footer options, and then click the Custom Footer button to open the Footer dialog box. The default footer, Page &[Page], is displayed in the Center Section box, instructing Excel to print the word *Page* followed by the page number as the footer.

6. Drag through Page &[Page], and press Delete to delete it. Then click OK. Excel returns to the Header/Footer options.

Centering on the page

7. Click the Margin tab to display its options. In the Center On Page section, click Horizontally and Vertically to center the worksheet horizontally and vertically on the page. The Preview box shows you the effects of your changes.

Turning off grid lines

8. Click the Sheet tab. Click the Gridlines check box to turn off that option, and then click OK. When you return to the Print Preview window, your worksheet looks like this:

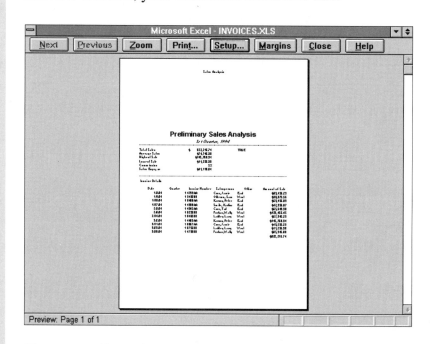

Page breaks

If you want to print the calculation area on one page and the supporting data on another, or if you need to control where the pages break in a multipage worksheet, select the cell below the row and to the right of the column at which you want Excel to break the page, and choose Page Break from the Insert menu. To remove a manual page break, select the cell immediately below and to the right of the page break, and choose Remove Page Break from the Insert menu. To remove all the page breaks in a worksheet, select the entire document by clicking the square in the top left corner of the worksheet (at the intersection of the row and column headers), and then choose Remove Page Break.

You can adjust the margins and column widths of your printout in the Print Preview window by clicking the Margins button to display guidelines and then manually moving the guidelines to increase or decrease the margins and columns.

9. When you're ready, click the Close button to return to the worksheet.

Preparing to Print

When you are ready to print, you can click the Print button on the Standard toolbar, or you can choose Print from the File menu to display this Print dialog box:

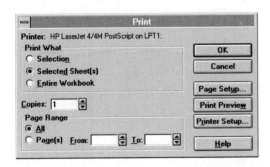

In this dialog box, you can adjust the print range and specify which pages you want to print in a multipage document. You can also go directly to the Page Setup dialog box by clicking the Page Setup button, or to Print Preview by clicking the Print Preview button.

To send the worksheet to the printer, you simply click OK. You can then evaluate the results of your efforts on paper.

Extracting Information from a List

What you will learn...

Create a pivot table to sum-marize worksheet data

Sum of Amount of Sale		Quarter				
Office	Salesperson	1	2	3	4	Grand Total
East	Crux, Jamie	$126,712.46	$126,712.46	$126,712.46	$126,712.46	$506,849.84
	Crux, Tad	$65,643.90	$65,643.90	$65,643.90	$65,643.90	$262,575.60
	Karnov, Peter	$209,225.17	$209,225.17	$209,225.17	$209,225.17	$836,900.68
	Smite, Karlina	$42,356.07	$42,356.07	$42,356.07	$42,356.07	$169,424.28
East Total		$443,937.60	$443,937.60	$443,937.60	$443,937.60	$1,775,750.40
West	Furban, Wally	$208,801.45	$208,801.45	$208,801.45	$208,801.45	$835,205.80
	Ladder, Larry	$78,602.13	$78,602.13	$78,602.13	$78,602.13	$314,408.52
	Olderon, Sam	$90,875.56	$90,875.56	$90,875.56	$90,875.56	$363,502.24
West Total		$378,279.14	$378,279.14	$378,279.14	$378,279.14	$1,513,116.56
Grand Total		$822,216.74	$822,216.74	$822,216.74	$822,216.74	$3,288,866.96

Center titles across columns for a professional look

Invoice Log
1993

Date	Quarter	Invoice Number	Salesperson	Office	Amount of Sale
1/3/94	1	4739AA	Crux, Jamie	East	$83,456.23
1/4/94	1	943200	Olderon, Sam	West	$90,875.56
1/10/94	1	8488AA	Karnov, Peter	East	$63,456.83
1/17/94	1	4398AA	Smite, Karlina	East	$42,356.07
2/3/94	1	4945AA	Crux, Tad	East	$65,643.90
2/8/94	1	825600	Furban, Wally	West	$123,456.45
2/14/94	1	846500	Ladder, Larry	West	$67,345.23
3/2/94	1	4409AA	Karnov, Peter	East	$145,768.34
3/11/94	1	8867AA	Crux, Jamie	East	$43,256.23
3/23/94	1	875600	Ladder, Larry	West	$11,256.90
3/30/94	1	479300	Furban, Wally	West	$85,345.00
4/5/94	2	4739AA	Crux, Jamie	East	$83,456.23
4/13/94	2	943200	Olderon, Sam	West	$90,875.56
4/21/94	2	8488AA	Karnov, Peter	East	$63,456.83
4/29/94	2	4398AA	Smite, Karlina	East	$42,356.07
5/7/94	2	4945AA	Crux, Tad	East	$65,643.90
5/15/94	2	825600	Furban, Wally	West	$123,456.45
5/23/94	2	846500	Ladder, Larry	West	$67,345.23
5/31/94	2	4409AA	Karnov, Peter	East	$145,768.34
6/8/94	2	8867AA	Crux, Jamie	East	$43,256.23
6/16/94	2	875600	Ladder, Larry	West	$11,256.90
6/24/94	2	479300	Furban, Wally	West	$85,345.00
7/4/94	3	4739AA	Crux, Jamie	East	$83,456.23
7/12/94	3	943200	Olderon, Sam	West	$90,875.56
7/20/94	3	8488AA	Karnov, Peter	East	$63,456.83
7/28/94	3	4398AA	Smite, Karlina	East	$42,356.07
8/5/94	3	4945AA	Crux, Tad	East	$65,643.90
8/13/94	3	825600	Furban, Wally	West	$123,456.45
8/21/94	3	846500	Ladder, Larry	West	$67,345.23
8/29/94	3	4409AA	Karnov, Peter	East	$145,768.34
9/6/94	3	8867AA	Crux, Jamie	East	$43,256.23
9/14/94	3	875600	Ladder, Larry	West	$11,256.90
9/22/94	3	479300	Furban, Wally	West	$85,345.00
10/3/94	4	4739AA	Crux, Jamie	East	$83,456.23
10/11/94	4	943200	Olderon, Sam	West	$90,875.56
10/19/94	4	8488AA	Karnov, Peter	East	$63,456.83
10/27/94	4	4398AA	Smite, Karlina	East	$42,356.07
11/4/94	4	4945AA	Crux, Tad	East	$65,643.90
11/12/94	4	825600	Furban, Wally	West	$123,456.45
11/20/94	4	846500	Ladder, Larry	West	$67,345.23
11/28/94	4	4409AA	Karnov, Peter	East	$145,768.34
12/6/94	4	8867AA	Crux, Jamie	East	$43,256.23
12/14/94	4	875600	Ladder, Larry	West	$11,256.90
12/22/94	4	479300	Furban, Wally	West	$85,345.00

Sort the data for easier analysis

Create a series of evenly spaced dates

The data in these columns is summarized in the pivot table

We covered a lot of important ground in Chapter 2, and you now have a feel for some of the power of Excel. In this chapter, we show you more techniques for efficient worksheet creation and management. Using an invoice log as a base worksheet, we describe how to sort and extract data and how to calculate statistics from a database, or *list*. If you have a database program such as Microsoft Access, you'll probably want to perform these tasks using that program's more sophisticated database tools. (*A Quick Course in Access*, another book in the Quick Course series, shows you how to create and manipulate databases with Microsoft Access.) But if you don't have a database program, you can carry out many database tasks with Excel.

We'll start by creating the invoice log for this example, and then we'll get down to business.

Cloning Worksheets

Using one worksheet as the basis for another is a very important time-saving technique. In this section, we will clone Sheet1 of the INVOICES workbook to create a worksheet in another workbook called INV_LOG. Then we'll use a few tricks to transform the new worksheet into a simulated invoice log (a record of sales). If you need to create such a log for your work, you can key in real data. In Chapter 6, we show you how to automate the process of inputting this kind of information so that you are spared hours of typing. In the meantime, though, let's create a simulated log to give us a large worksheet to manipulate in this chapter. Follow these steps to create INV_LOG:

1. Click the Open button or choose Open from the File menu to display the Open dialog box. Double-click the EXAMPLES directory. The files stored in the EXCEL\EXAMPLES directory appear in the File Name list. Select INVOICES.XLS and then click OK to open the INVOICES workbook.

2. Choose Save As from the File menu to display the Save As dialog box.

3. In the File Name edit box, type *inv_log* and click OK. You have two identical workbooks saved under different names.

A few alterations to INV_LOG will give you a usable sample worksheet. Remember to save your work frequently as you follow the steps in the next sections.

1. In cell A1, type *Invoice Log* and press Enter to enter the text in A1 and move down one cell. In cell A2, type *'1993* and press Enter.

2. Select the headers for rows 3 through 12, right-click them to display the row shortcut menu, and then choose Delete to remove the selected rows.

3. Select A5:F15, click the Copy button, click cell A16, and click the Paste button to insert the selected range of data.

4. Select A5:F26, click the Copy button, click cell A27, and click the Paste button to insert the selected range of data.

Now, so that the log includes invoices for all the months of the year, follow these steps:

1. Select cell A16, type *4/5/94*, and click the Confirm button. Excel displays the new date for this invoice and then recalculates the formula in cell B16, assigning the invoice to the second quarter of the year instead of the first.

Rather than changing dates manually for the rest of the worksheet, we'll take this opportunity to demonstrate the Fill and Series commands on the Edit menu. In a moment, we'll use this command to create a sequential set of numbers. Here, we'll use it to create a set of evenly spaced dates. (Obviously, if you were logging real invoices in this database, you would use the actual sale dates.)

2. Select A16:A26 and choose Fill and then Series from the Edit menu. Excel displays this dialog box:

← Creating a series of evenly spaced dates

Automatic date series

You can use AutoFill to create a series of dates. Simply enter the starting date and drag the fill handle through the range you want to fill. Excel assumes you want to create a series with a step value of one day. To fill a range with the same date, without creating a series, hold down the Ctrl key while dragging the fill handle.

3. Because the value in cell A16 is a date, Excel assumes you want to create a set of dates. Type *8* in the Step Value box, and then click OK. Excel uses the value in cell A16 as its starting point and creates a series of dates that are eight days apart. (To create a series that skips to Monday if a date falls on Saturday or Sunday, click the Weekday option before clicking OK.)

4. Select cell A27, type *7/4/94*, and click the Confirm button.

Repeating a command 5. Select A27:A37 and choose Repeat Fill from the Edit menu.

6. Select cell A38, type *10/3/94*, and click the Confirm button.

7. Select A38:A48 and this time, click the Repeat button on the Standard toolbar. Your worksheet now contains 43 rows of information.

8. Press Ctrl+Home and then scroll through the worksheet. The formulas in column B have done their work and assigned the invoices to quarters based on the dates in column A.

This large worksheet is ideal for demonstrating some of Excel's list capabilities.

Sorting Data

A step value other than 1

To use AutoFill to create a series with a step value other than 1, enter the first and second values in the series, select both values, and drag the fill handle through the range in which you want the series to appear. The second value tells Excel what to use as a step value. For example, entering 1 and 3 tells Excel to create a series with a step value of 3. (To create a series of numbers using Auto-Fill, you must enter two values; if you enter only one, Excel simply fills the range with the starting value.)

The sales data in the worksheet you created in Chapter 2 fits neatly on one screen. To find out which salesperson from the West office has made the highest single sale, you could simply look at the worksheet. Getting that information from the worksheet now on your screen is a little more difficult. Fortunately, Excel can quickly sort worksheets like this one, using one, two, or more levels of sorting.

Adding Sort Codes

Before you sort any large worksheet, you should ask yourself whether you might need to put the data back in its original order. If there is even a chance that you will, you should add sort codes to the worksheet before you begin sorting. A *sort code* is a sequential number assigned to each row of entries.

After changing the order of the entries, you can sort again on the basis of the sort code to put everything back where it was. Follow these steps to add sort codes to the invoice log:

1. Right-click the header of column A to display the column shortcut menu and choose Insert to insert a blank column in front of the Date column.

2. Select cell A4, type *Sort Code*, and press Enter.

3. In cell A5, type *1* and click the Confirm button.

Creating a series of numbers

4. Select A5:A48 and choose Fill and then Series from the Edit menu.

5. The default settings—Columns as the Series In option, Linear as the Type option, and a Step Value of 1—will produce the result you want, so click OK. Excel uses the value in cell A5 as its starting point and inserts a sequential set of numbers in the selected range, as shown here:

	A	B	C	D	E	F	
4	Sort Code	Date	Quarter	Invoice Number	Salesperson	Office	Amc
5	1	1/3/94	1	4739AA	Crux, Jamie	East	
6	2	1/4/94	1	943200	Olderon, Sam	West	
7	3	1/10/94	1	8488AA	Karnov, Peter	East	
8	4	1/17/94	1	4398AA	Smite, Karlina	East	
9	5	2/3/94	1	4945AA	Crux, Tad	East	
10	6	2/8/94	1	825600	Furban, Wally	West	
11	7	2/14/94	1	846500	Ladder, Larry	West	
12	8	3/2/94	1	4409AA	Karnov, Peter	East	
13	9	3/11/94	1	8867AA	Crux, Jamie	East	
14	10	3/23/94	1	875600	Ladder, Larry	West	
15	11	3/30/94	1	479300	Furban, Wally	West	
16	12	4/5/94	2	4739AA	Crux, Jamie	East	
17	13	4/13/94	2	943200	Olderon, Sam	West	
18	14	4/21/94	2	8488AA	Karnov, Peter	East	
19	15	4/29/94	2	4398AA	Smite, Karlina	East	
20	16	5/7/94	2	4945AA	Crux, Tad	East	
21	17	5/15/94	2	825600	Furban, Wally	West	

Now let's look at various ways you might want to sort Sheet1 of the INV_LOG workbook.

Using One Sort Column

The simplest sorting procedure is based on only one column. You indicate which column Excel should use, and the program rearranges the rows of the selected range accordingly. Let's start by sorting the data in INV_LOG by regional office so that you can see how the process works:

1. Select A5:G48 and choose Sort from the Data menu. Excel displays the Sort dialog box in which you can select three different sorting columns. Excel automatically enters the first column in the selection in the Sort By edit box:

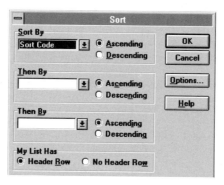

2. You want Excel to use the Office column as the basis for a one-column sort, so click the down arrow to the right of the Sort By edit box to drop down a list of the columns in the selection. Click the bottom scroll arrow to scroll the list, and then select Office.

3. By default, Excel selects Ascending as the sort order for the records. Click OK to sort the records with the current settings.

The invoice data is now sorted alphabetically by regional office, with all the invoices for the East office coming before those for the West office.

Using Two Sort Columns

Now let's take things a step further and sort the invoices not only by regional office but also by salesperson:

1. With the range still highlighted, choose Sort from the Data menu. The previous sort column, Office, is still entered in the Sort By edit box.

Sorting buttons

Two sorting buttons, located on the Standard toolbar, can be used when you are sorting data based on only one column. Tell Excel which column is the sort column by clicking a cell in that column before using the sorting button. Then click the Sort Ascending button to sort the list from A to Z or the Sort Descending button to sort from Z to A. Excel then sorts the list in which the cell you selected is located.

2. To add a second sort column, click the down arrow to the right of the first Then By edit box, select Salesperson, and click OK.

The invoice log is now sorted alphabetically by regional office and alphabetically within region by the names of the salespeople.

Using Three Sort Columns

Depending on the focus of your current analysis, you might want to sort INV_LOG based on the Date or Quarter columns. However, let's assume you are interested in each person's sales volume and add one more column to the sort. To sort by regional office, salesperson, and amount of invoice, follow these steps:

1. Choose Sort from the Data menu. Again, the Sort dialog box retains the selections from the previous sort.

2. Click the down arrow to the right of the second Then By edit box, select Amount of Sale, and click OK.

3. Press Ctrl+Home and then adjust the widths of columns B, C, and F so that columns A through G are visible. Here are the results (we've scrolled the screen a little):

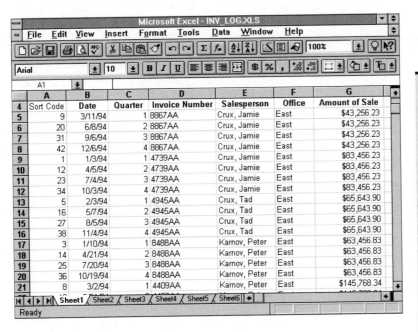

Sorting by columns

If your worksheet has labels down the leftmost column instead of across the top row and your data is oriented horizontally instead of vertically, you will want to sort by columns instead of rows. In the Sort dialog box, click the Options button to display the Sort Options dialog box. Then in the Orientation section, select Sort Left To Right and click OK. Select the list and then click OK again to sort the data.

Keeping Headings in View

You can now scroll through the invoice log to check how Excel has sorted the data. As you scroll, you'll probably wish that the column headings didn't scroll out of sight. You can keep the headings at the top of the screen like this:

1. Scroll the worksheet so that row 4—the row with the column headings—is at the top of your screen.

Splitting the window into panes

2. Move the mouse pointer to the black bar, called the split bar, at the top of the right scroll bar.

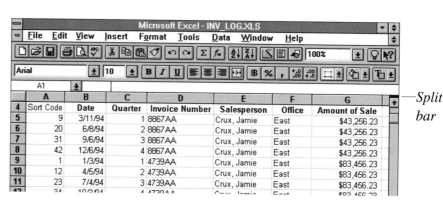

Split bar

3. When the pointer changes into a set of double lines with opposing arrows, drag the split bar down between rows 4 and 5:

Synchronized scrolling

If you split the worksheet window horizontally and then use the bottom scroll bar to scroll the window, both panes of the window scroll so that columns always align. Likewise, if you split the worksheet window vertically and then use the right scroll bar, the rows scroll simultaneously.

You can also use the split bar at the right end of the bottom scroll bar to split the window vertically. You can even split the window both horizontally and vertically using the split bars. Alternatively, you can use the Split command on the Window menu. When you choose this command, Excel splits the window above and to the left of the selected cell.

4. Use the scroll bar for the lower windowpane to scroll the sorted data while the column labels remain visible in the upper windowpane.

Scrolling split windows

5. When you finish viewing the data, restore the single pane by dragging the split bar back up to its original position at the top of the right scroll bar, by double-clicking the split bar, or by choosing Remove Split from the Window menu.

Removing the panes

List Basics

The invoice log is an organized collection of information about invoices. By common definition, it is a *database*, known in Excel 5 as a *list*. A list is a table of related data with a rigid structure that enables you to easily locate and evaluate individual items of information. Each row of a list is a *record* that contains all the pertinent information about one component of the list. For example, row 5 of the invoice log contains all the information about one particular invoice. Each cell of the list is a *field* that contains one item of information. Cell G5, for example, contains the amount of the invoice for the record in row 5. All the fields in a particular column contain the same kind of information about their respective records. For example, column B of the invoice log contains the dates of all the invoices. At the top of each column is a heading, called the *field name*.

Lists

Records

Fields

In the next sections, we'll cover Excel's list capabilities. First, however, follow these steps to restore the invoice log to its original order and to make a few other necessary adjustments:

1. Select A5:G48 and choose Sort from the Data menu to display the Sort dialog box. Click the down arrow to the right of the Sort By edit box and select Sort Code. For each of the two Then By edit boxes click the down arrows and select (none) from the drop-down list. Then click OK. Excel sorts the records back into their original order.

2. Right-click the column A header to display the column short-cut menu and choose Delete. The invoice log now contains only its original six columns.

Freezing panes

You can use Freeze Panes on the Window menu to lock rows, columns, or both so that you can then keep column or row headings in view while you scroll other portions of the worksheet. To freeze a row or rows, select the row above which you want to make the freeze and choose Freeze Panes from the Window menu. Similarly, to freeze a column or columns, select the column to the left of which you want to make the freeze and then choose the command. Selecting a single cell and choosing the command freezes the rows above and columns to the left of the selected cell. Choose Unfreeze Panes to unfreeze the frozen windowpanes.

The data form ———————→

You are now ready to begin exploring Excel's list operations, which you perform by choosing the Form command from the Data menu to display a dialog box called a *data form*. As you'll see in the following sections, the options in the data form provide ways to find, add, delete, and modify records. Before choosing the Form command, you must select the first cell of the list. Follow these steps to display the data form:

1. Select cell A5 and choose Form from the Data menu. This data form appears:

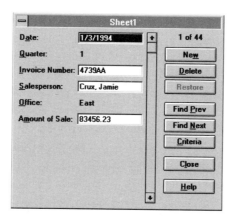

As you can see, the name of the sheet appears in the title bar of the dialog box. The column headings have become the field names and are displayed down the left side of the form. One record's data is displayed in the edit boxes adjacent to the field names. If a field contains a formula, as the Quarter field does, the data form displays the results of the formula, not the formula itself. The result is not in an edit box, indicating that you can't edit the field.

Data form size

Excel can display up to 32 fields on a data form. If your list has over 32 fields, when you choose Form from the Data menu to display a data form, Excel tells you that your list has too many fields. Reduce the number of fields and try again. (A quick way to reduce the number of fields without losing data is to insert a blank column after the 32nd field.)

Finding Records

The data form allows you to find records by stepping through the list one record at a time or by entering criteria to identify specific records. Let's step through the list first:

1. Click the Find Next button in the data form. Excel displays the second record. The numbers in the top right corner show how many records are in the list and which record is currently displayed.

2. Click the Find Next and Find Prev buttons to step back and forth through the list. When you are finished, use the scroll bar to the right of the fields or the command buttons to move to record 1.

You use the Criteria button in the data form to find a specific record or records in the list, like this:

1. Click the Criteria button to display the criteria form, which resembles a blank data form.

The criteria form

2. To find all invoices over $85,000 for Wally Furban, type *Furban, Wally* in the Salesperson edit box and *>85000* in the Amount of Sale edit box, as shown here:

Entering criteria

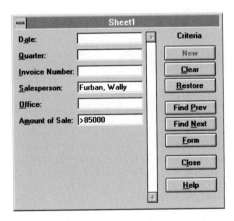

3. Click the Find Next button. Excel moves you back to the data form with the first record in the list that meets the criteria displayed. Click the Find Next button again, and Excel displays the next record that meets the criteria. You can continue clicking the Find Next button until you reach the end of the list. Move back through the records by clicking the Find Prev button.

4. Return to the criteria form by clicking the Criteria button and then remove the criteria by clicking the Clear button.

5. Move back to the data form by clicking the Form button. All records are now accessible.

Comparison operators and wildcards

You can use these comparison operators to compute criteria:

= > < >= <= <>

and you can specify wildcards, using the standard DOS wildcards * and ? for matching text. For example, specifying *Crux,** as the Salesperson would locate the records for both Jamie Crux and Tad Crux.

Adding and Deleting Records

The data form can be used to add and delete records from the list. As an example, we'll add a new record, find it, and then remove it from the list. Follow these steps:

Filling in a blank data form

1. With the data form displayed on your screen, click the New button. Excel clears the fields of the data form so that you can type the information for a new record. New Record is displayed in the top right corner.

2. Fill in the record with the following data using the Tab key to move from field to field:

Date	11/2/94
Invoice Number	4980AA
Salesperson	Crux, Jamie
Amount of Sale	59500

Because Quarter and Office are calculated fields, you don't need to enter anything for those fields. The data form now looks like this:

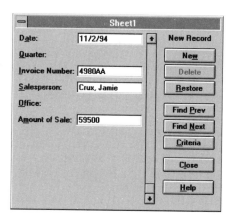

Restore Button

When you are editing a record in the data form, you can restore the previous data by clicking the Restore button. This button works only if you haven't yet moved to another record or pressed the Enter key.

3. Click the New button or press Enter to add the record to the invoice log. (Excel adds new records to the end of a list.)

4. Click the Find Prev button. Excel displays the record you just added—record 45. Notice that the calculated fields now have data in them.

5. With the new record still displayed, click the Delete button. Excel warns you that the record will be permanently deleted.

6. Click OK. Excel deletes the record and displays the data form for a new record.

7. Click the Find Prev button again. The last record in the list is again record 44.

8. Click Close to remove the data form from the screen and return to your worksheet.

Filtering Records

Suppose you invested a considerable chunk of your advertising budget for the year on a direct-mail flyer about a two-week promotion. For another two-week promotion earlier in the year, you relied on your salespeople to get the word out to their customers. You want to compare sales during the two promotions. Or suppose you want to analyze all sales over $60,000 to see if you can detect sales patterns. In either case, you can tell Excel to extract all the relevant invoices for scrutiny. You give Excel instructions of this kind by choosing Filter and then AutoFilter from the Data menu and then defining filtering criteria. To see how AutoFilter works, follow these steps:

AutoFilter

1. With row 4 at the top of your screen and cell A5 selected, choose Filter and then AutoFilter from the Data menu. Excel displays down arrows for each field, like this:

	A	B	C	D	E	F	G
4	Date	Quarte	Invoice Numb	Salesperso	Office	Amount of Sal	
5	1/3/94	1	4739AA	Crux, Jamie	East	$83,456.23	
6	1/4/94	1	943200	Olderon, Sam	West	$90,875.56	
7	1/10/94	1	8488AA	Karnov, Peter	East	$63,456.83	
8	1/17/94	1	4398AA	Smite, Karlina	East	$42,356.07	
9	2/3/94	1	4945AA	Crux, Tad	East	$65,643.90	
10	2/8/94	1	825600	Furban, Wally	West	$123,456.45	
11	2/14/94	1	846500	Ladder, Larry	West	$67,345.23	
12	3/2/94	1	4409AA	Karnov, Peter	East	$145,768.34	
13	3/11/94	1	8867AA	Crux, Jamie	East	$43,256.23	

2. Click the down arrow for the Quarter field. Excel displays a list of the unique values in the Quarter field—1, 2, 3, and 4—as well as four other options—All, Custom, Blanks, and NonBlanks.

3. Click the down arrow for the Salesperson field. Again, Excel displays a list of the unique names in the field and the four other options.

4. Select Karnov, Peter. Excel immediately filters out all the records for Peter, hiding the other records:

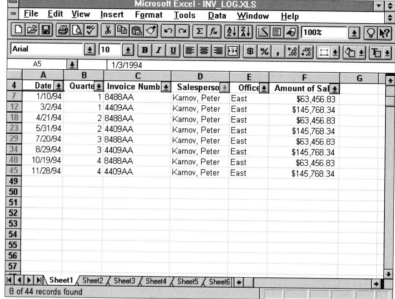

Notice that Excel retains the original record numbers and changes the color of the down arrow for the Salesperson field to indicate which column is being used for filtering. Excel displays the results of the filter operation—*8 of 44 records found*—in the status bar.

Suppose you want to see Peter Karnov's records for the second quarter only. Try this:

1. Click the down arrow for the Quarter field and select 2. Now only the second quarter records for Peter are displayed.

2. To display all of Peter's records again, click the down arrow for the Quarter field and select (All).

Customizing Filters

Now let's get a little fancy. Suppose you want to see only the records for Peter Karnov with amounts over $70,000. To filter out these records, you use the Custom option on the drop-down list. Follow these steps:

1. Click the down arrow for the Amount of Sale field and select (Custom) to display this Custom AutoFilter dialog box:

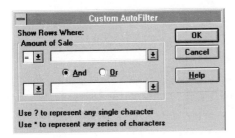

In this dialog box, you can use operators and the And or Or buttons to set criteria for the Amount of Sale field.

2. Click the down arrow to the right of the = sign to display a list of operators, and then select > (the greater than operator).

Using operators in filters

3. Press the Tab key to move to the adjacent criteria box and type *70000*.

4. Click OK. Excel selects the records and displays these results:

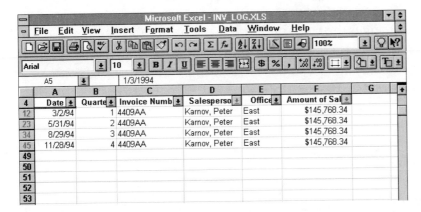

You can remove all the filters you've set up so far by choosing Filter and then Show All from the Data menu. You can then apply different filters to the entire list. As another example, let's filter out the first and third quarter invoices from the list by using the Or button in the Custom AutoFilter dialog box.

1. Choose Filter and then Show All from the Data menu. Excel displays all the records in the database.

Removing filters

2. Click the down arrow for the Quarter field and select Custom.

Using multiple filters

3. In the Custom AutoFilter dialog box, leave = as the operator and type *1* as the first criteria. Then click the Or button, select = as the operator, and type *3* as the second criteria. The dialog box looks like this:

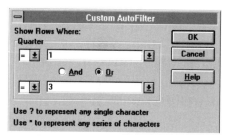

4. Click OK to display these results:

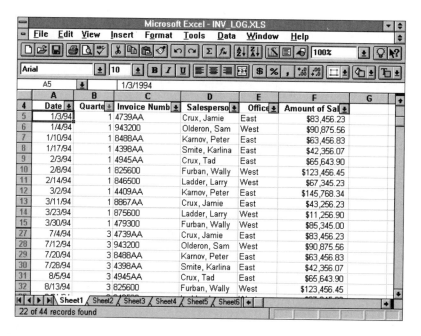

Turning off AutoFilter

5. Turn off filtering by choosing Filter from the Data menu and then choosing AutoFilter from the submenu to deactivate it. Excel displays all the records again.

The filtering of records allows you to act on these records without affecting the other records in your database. For example, you can change the font of filtered records or sort them. You can also create a chart using the data from filtered records (see page 94 for information about charts).

Summarizing Data

Often you will want to summarize the data in a list in some way—for example, by totaling sets of entries. Excel's new PivotTable Wizard allows you to do just that. The Wizard walks you through the steps of creating a *pivot table* with the type of summary calculation you specify. After you create the pivot table, you can reformat it by "pivoting" rows and columns on the screen to provide different views of the data.

The PivotTable Wizard

Let's use the invoice log to build a pivot table, and then we'll modify the table. First display the Query And Pivot toolbar by following these steps:

1. Right-click anywhere on a toolbar to display the toolbar short-cut menu, and choose Toolbars to display this dialog box:

Displaying the Query And Pivot toolbar

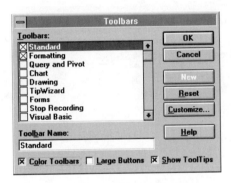

2. Click the Query And Pivot option in the Toolbars list and click OK. Excel displays a floating Query And Pivot toolbar.

3. Drag the toolbar up until its outline is over the name box and the left end of the formula bar. When you release the mouse button, the toolbar snaps into place, like this:

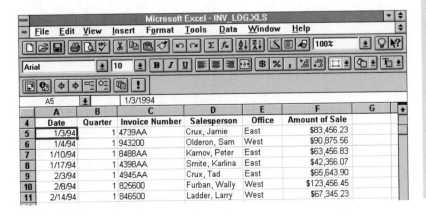

Microsoft Query

Excel ships with a program called Microsoft Query that you can use to access data in files that were created with database programs such as Paradox, dBASE, Microsoft Access, and Microsoft Fox-Pro. For more information, see *Querying Databases with Microsoft Excel*, one of the manuals in the Excel package.

4. Take a moment to point to each button so that ToolTips can give you some idea of what the buttons do.

Creating the Pivot Table

We will start by building a pivot table that summarizes the quarterly data for each salesperson by totaling the quarterly amounts and each salesperson's amounts. Follow these steps:

1. Click the PivotTable Wizard button to display the first of the Wizard's four dialog boxes:

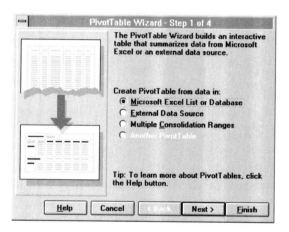

2. Click Next to create a pivot table from the INV_LOG list. Excel displays this Step 2 dialog box:

Naming lists

If you know you will add data to a list from which you are constructing a pivot table, assign a name to the list and enter that name in the Range edit box of the Step 2 dialog box. Then any data you add will be included in future versions of the pivot table without your having to go back and adjust the range.

3. Excel has already entered the range containing the invoice information—A4:F48—in the Range edit box, so click Next to display the Step 3 dialog box, where you set up the pivot table layout by dragging the necessary fields to the appropriate areas.

4. Drag the Salesperson field button to the ROW area, drag the Quarter field button to the COLUMN area, and then drag the Amount of Sale button to the DATA area. By default, Excel will calculate the sum of the Amount of Sale data. The dialog box looks like this:

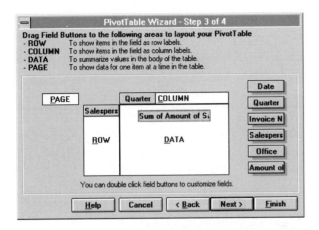

5. Click Next to display the Step 4 dialog box. Scroll the worksheet so that column H is visible to the right of the dialog box and click cell H4. Excel enters an absolute reference to cell H4 of Sheet1 in the Starting Cell edit box, as shown here:

Specifying the pivot table's location

6. Click Finish to accept the default options and then scroll the screen to the right to see the new pivot table, which Excel has created in H4:M13:

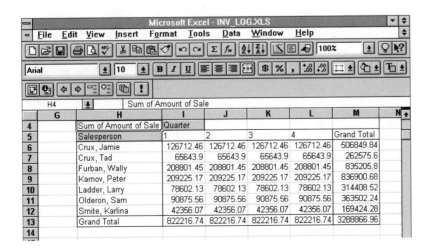

Excel has totaled the invoices by employee and by quarter, and has also calculated yearly totals for each employee and quarterly totals for the entire sales force.

Modifying the Pivot Table

Now that you have built a basic table, you can easily modify it with a variety of tools that Excel provides. Let's start by adding a field to the PAGE area of the table. The PAGE area allows you to filter the data in the table—for example, you can see only the East office's data or only the West office's data. Here's how:

Filtering the data

1. Click the PivotTable Wizard button. Excel displays the Step 3 dialog box with the current pivot table's settings.

2. Drag the Office field button to the PAGE area and then click Finish.

3. Scroll the pivot table downward. Excel has added the Office field above the table, together with a filter—currently set to All—that allows you to view the data in different ways:

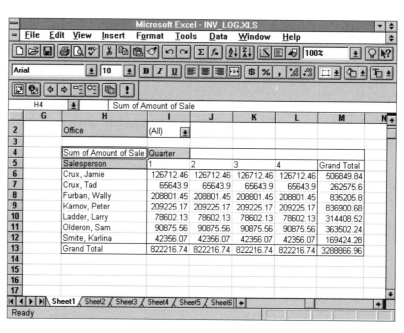

Updating pivot tables

If you change the data in a list that is the source for a pivot table, you can update the pivot table to reflect the new data by clicking the Refresh Table button on the Query And Pivot toolbar or by choosing the Refresh Data command from the Data menu.

4. Click the filter's down arrow and select East from the drop-down list to display the totals for only the East office. Repeat this step for the West office, and then select All to redisplay the totals for both offices.

You can change the type of calculation for the Amount of Sale field by using either of two buttons: the PivotTable Wizard button or the PivotTable Field button. We'll use first one and then the other:

1. Click the PivotTable Wizard button to display the Wizard's Step 3 dialog box.

Changing the type of calculation

2. Double-click Sum Of Amount Of Sales in the DATA area to display this dialog box:

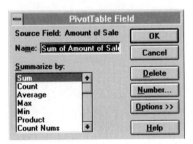

3. Select Count from the Summarized By list and click OK. The DATA area now indicates that Count Of Amount Of Sale is the calculation option.

4. Click Finish to return to the worksheet, where the pivot table now looks like this:

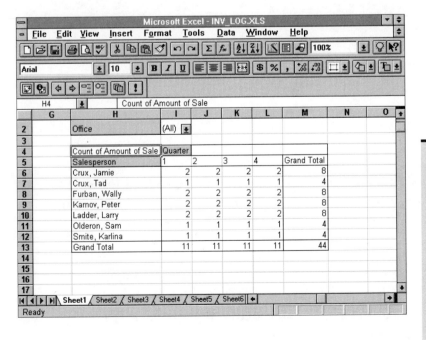

Adding and deleting fields

To add a field to a pivot table, select a cell in the table and click the PivotTable Wizard button to display the Step 3 dialog box. Then drag the field button for the new field to the appropriate area. To delete a field, simply drag the field away from the table.

5. To total the invoice amounts again, check that cell H4, Count Of Amount Of Sale, is selected and click the PivotTable Field button to display the PivotTable Field dialog box. Select Sum from the Summarized By list, but don't click OK yet.

Formatting the pivot table

6. To format the values in the pivot table, click the Number button to display the Format Cells dialog box, select the Currency category, select the third format from the Format Codes list, and click OK twice. Excel totals the invoices by salesperson and by quarter. (Obviously the results obtained from our cloned worksheet are not very enlightening!) Excel displays the results in dollars and cents and adjusts the column widths to accommodate the new values, as shown here:

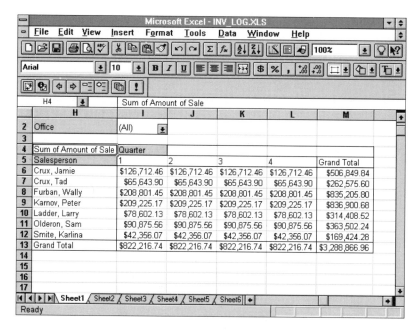

You can also manipulate the data by moving the fields on the worksheet. You can drag any field in the pivot table to any area to produce almost instantly any summarized format you choose. For example, suppose you want to see the total amount for each office and for each salesperson within each office. You can combine the Office and Salesperson fields in the ROW area, like this:

Moving the fields

1. Point to cell H2 and drag the Office field down and to the left of cell H5, which contains the Salesperson field. Excel calculates the data for both fields, as shown here:

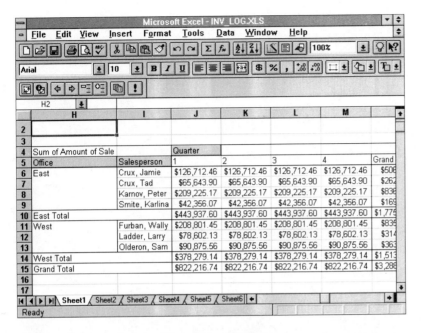

2. Turn off the Query And Pivot toolbar by right-clicking any toolbar, choosing Toolbars from the shortcut menu, deselecting Query And Pivot in the Toolbars list, and clicking OK.

3. Press Ctrl+Home and click the Save button to save the INV_LOG workbook.

In this chapter, we've only scratched the surface as far as pivot tables in particular and lists in general are concerned. As you use these features, you'll find that they can make light work of extraction and summarization, perhaps encouraging you to tackle tasks that would otherwise seem too intimidating, cumbersome, or time-consuming.

Visually Presenting Data

What you will learn...

*Instantly format a work-
sheet with an autoformat*

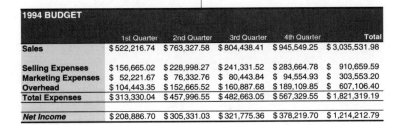

1994 BUDGET					
	1st Quarter	2nd Quarter	3rd Quarter	4th Quarter	Total
Sales	$ 522,216.74	$ 763,327.58	$ 804,438.41	$ 945,549.25	$ 3,035,531.98
Selling Expenses	$ 156,665.02	$ 228,998.27	$ 241,331.52	$ 283,664.78	$ 910,659.59
Marketing Expenses	$ 52,221.67	$ 76,332.76	$ 80,443.84	$ 94,554.93	$ 303,553.20
Overhead	$ 104,443.35	$ 152,665.52	$ 160,887.68	$ 189,109.85	$ 607,106.40
Total Expenses	$ 313,330.04	$ 457,996.55	$ 482,663.05	$ 567,329.55	$ 1,821,319.19
Net Income	$ 208,886.70	$ 305,331.03	$ 321,775.36	$ 378,219.70	$ 1,214,212.79

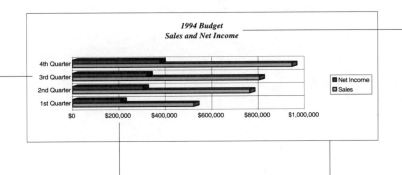

*Easily add and
format a title*

*Plot data with
the help of
ChartWizard*

*Scale the axes to
maximize legibility*

*Frame the chart to anchor
it on the page*

I n the previous chapters, you learned a lot about Excel, and you can now put Excel to use in your own work. After all that effort, let's relax a bit in this chapter. Using a budget worksheet as a basis, we'll explore various ways you can visually present your worksheet data.

Setting Up a Budget

Before we can start, we need to set up this projected budget worksheet:

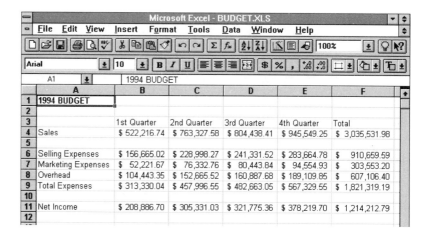

Once the worksheet is in place, we can plot the budget information as various kinds of charts. Assuming that you have started Windows and Excel, follow these steps to create the worksheet:

1. Close any open workbooks by choosing Close from the File menu or by clicking the workbook's Control menu icon—the gray box with the small fat hyphen at the left end of the menu bar. Then click the New Workbook button on the toolbar. If necessary, click the Maximize button to expand the workbook window to fill the available space.

2. Save the blank workbook in the EXCEL\EXAMPLES directory as BUDGET.XLS, and if you want, fill out the Summary Info dialog box. From now on, save the workbook frequently as you build the budget.

3. In cell A1, type *1994 BUDGET*, click the Confirm button to enter the title, and click the Bold button to make the title bold.

4. In cell B3, type *1st Quarter* and click the Confirm button. Using AutoFill, drag the fill handle to cell E3 (see page 57 for more information about AutoFill). Excel automatically fills the range with the labels 2nd Quarter, 3rd Quarter, and 4th Quarter. Finally, enter *Total* in cell F3.

Filling cells with a series of labels

5. In cell A4, type *Sales* and press Right Arrow.

6. Next, enter these sales amounts in the indicated cells:

B4	522216.74
C4	763327.58
D4	804438.41
E4	945549.25

Now let's tackle the expenses. To simplify the data entry process for this example, let's assume that we have selling expenses that average 30 percent of sales, marketing expenses that average 10 percent of sales, and overhead expenses (fixed costs) that average 20 percent.

1. Enter the following information in the indicated cells:

A6	Selling Expenses
A7	Marketing Expenses
A8	Overhead
A9	Total Expenses
A11	Net Income
B6	=.3*B4
B7	=.1*B4
B8	=.2*B4
B9	=SUM(B6:B8)

For the entry in cell B9, you can either enter the SUM function from the keyboard, or you can click the AutoSum button.

2. Select B6:B9 and drag the fill handle across to column E to duplicate the 1st quarter formulas for the 2nd, 3rd, and 4th quarters.

More about AutoFill

You can copy information from one area of your worksheet to another using two methods: Auto-Fill, and copy and paste. These methods produce similar results unless the entry you are copying contains a number that can be incremented, such as in the 1st Quarter heading, or the cell contains an entry from a custom list. If the cell contains a number that can be incremented, using Auto-Fill copies the entry and increments the number—for example, 1st Quarter becomes 2nd Quarter, 3rd Quarter, and so on. If the cell contains an entry from a custom list, Excel fills the cells with other entries from that list. You define a custom list by choosing Options from the Tools menu, clicking the Custom Lists tab, clicking NEW in the Custom Lists box, and typing the list's entries in the List Entries box. (You can also select a range containing the entries and click the Import button to import the entries as a list.) After you click OK, you can enter the list in consecutive cells of any worksheet by typing one of the entries and dragging the fill handle. This feature is invaluable if you frequently create worksheets involving lists of the same entries, such as part numbers or employee names.

3. Select B4:F11 and click the Currency Style button on the Formatting toolbar.

4. Widen column A so that all its labels are visible. Then drag through the headers for columns B through E and choose Column and then Width from the Format menu. When the Column Width dialog box appears, type *12* in the Column Width edit box, and click OK. All four selected columns take on the new width.

Now, let's compute the Total column and Net Income row:

1. In cell B11, type =*B4–B9* and click the Confirm button. Excel enters the result, $208,886.70, as the 1st Quarter's net income.

2. Use AutoFill to copy the formula in cell B11 to C11:F11.

3. Select cell F4, click the AutoSum button, and click the Confirm button.

4. Widen column F as needed.

5. Point to the bottom border of cell F4, hold down Ctrl, and drag the cell image to F6. When you release the mouse button, Excel copies the SUM function to the specified location.

6. Use AutoFill to copy the formula in cell F6 to F7:F9.

Voilà! Your worksheet should look like the one shown earlier.

Fancy Formatting

You have seen that you can use combinations of fonts and styles to draw attention to important worksheet details. Now let's look at a powerful Excel feature designed to make short work of worksheet formatting: *autoformats*. An autoformat is a predefined combination of formatting that works well with worksheets like the one we just created to produce fancy-looking reports with the click of a button. Try this:

1. Select A1:F11 and choose AutoFormat from the Format menu. Excel displays this dialog box:

Outlining worksheets

Excel's outlining feature lets you view as little or as much of a worksheet as you want to see. To outline a worksheet, select all the cells containing data, and choose Group And Outline and then Auto Outline from the Data menu. Excel searches for what it considers to be the most important information (for example, the totals) and uses this information to create different row and column outline levels. Initially, an outlined worksheet displays all its levels. You use the row level buttons and column level buttons in the top left corner of the window to expand and collapse the outline. For example, clicking the 2 row level button displays only the first and second levels and hides any lower levels. You can also click the Hide Detail buttons (marked with minus signs) above and to the left of the worksheet to collapse an outline level. Excel deduces that the last row or column of a section is the "bottom line" of the collapsed section and displays only that row or column. Conversely, you can click the Show Detail buttons (marked with plus signs) to expand collapsed levels. Choose Group And Outline and then Clear Outline to leave outline mode.

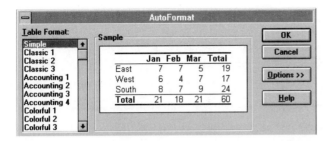

2. In the Table Format list, find and select 3D Effects 1 and click
   OK. Here's the impressive result:

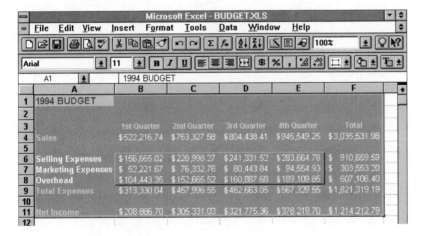

3. Click the Print button to print the budget data.

4. Now choose AutoFormat from the Format menu again, select
   Colorful 2 from the Table Format list, and click OK to
   produce another eye-catching report.

5. Try some of the other autoformats, finishing with Classic 2.

The autoformats that come with Excel don't work well unless
your worksheet is set up with them in mind. Nevertheless,
they are a great way to become familiar with the many effects
you can create with combinations of fonts, lines, colors, and
shading. If you don't find a format that produces exactly the
look you want, you can assign an autoformat as a starting
point and then make refinements using the Font, Color, Font
Color, and Borders buttons or the options available in the
Format Cells dialog box.

Removing worksheet autoformats

If you decide not to use a worksheet autoformat after all, choose
AutoFormat from the Format
menu, select None from the Table
Format list, and click OK.

Plotting Charts

With Excel, you can create charts in three ways: on the current worksheet, as a separate sheet in the current workbook, or in another workbook. In this section, we show you how to quickly plot data on the current worksheet. The advantage of this method is that you can then print the chart and the underlying worksheet on the same page. We'll create the chart using ChartWizard, which automates the otherwise complex process of creating and then formatting charts. Don't be concerned if your chart doesn't look exactly the same as our chart. Differences in screen setups or the order of selecting functions can change the way charts display.

ChartWizard

When you create a chart from a selected range of data in a worksheet, Excel maintains a link between the worksheet and the chart. This link is dynamic: If you make changes to the worksheet data, Excel revises the chart to reflect the new data. You can create more than one chart from the same range of data, and the data can be arranged either in columns or rows. The first chart we'll create is a column-oriented chart.

1. Select A6:E8 and click the ChartWizard button.

2. Move the cross-hair pointer to the blank area below your budget, hold down the mouse button, and drag to create a *marquee*—a dotted box—about the size of the worksheet window. (Don't worry about the precise size and location for now.) Then release the mouse button. ChartWizard displays the first of five dialog boxes to lead you through the process of creating and customizing a chart:

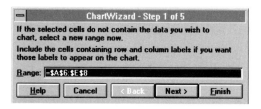

3. Click Next, both to confirm that you want Excel to plot the range you selected and to move to the next dialog box:

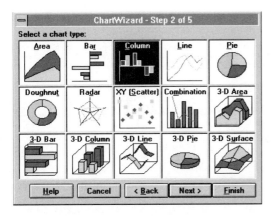

4. Select 3-D Column as the chart format, and then click Next to display this dialog box:

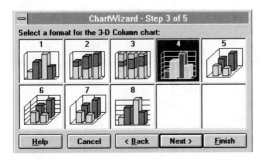

5. Accept the default 3-D column type by clicking Next. Excel displays in the fourth dialog box how the selected range will look as a chart, with all labels and other information in place:

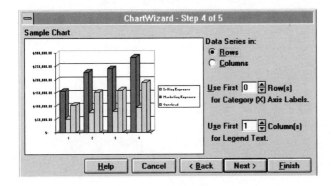

6. Accept the default settings and move to the next dialog box by clicking Next. (At any point in the chart-creating process, you can click the Back button to move back to a previous dialog box, so you can always select a different format if you change your mind.)

Creating charts on chart sheets

To create a chart on a separate chart sheet, first select the data and then click the ChartWizard button. Next choose Chart from the Insert menu and select the As New Sheet option. Excel places a sheet named Chart1 in front of the worksheet and displays the first ChartWizard dialog box. Now build the chart in the Chart-Wizard's dialog boxes as usual. Excel places the results on the Chart1 sheet. To quickly build a chart in the default format on a separate chart sheet, simply select the worksheet data you want to plot and press the F11 key.

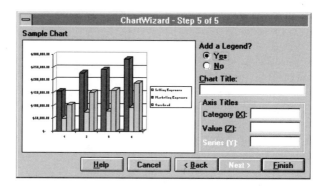

7. In the final dialog box, accept the default settings for a legend and click Finish. Excel displays the Chart toolbar and plots this chart:

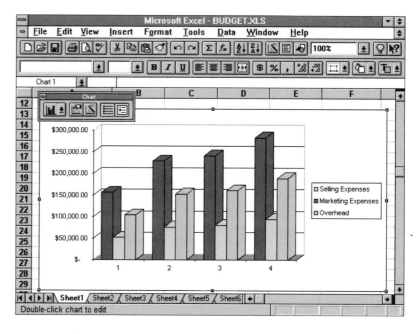

As you can see, four groups of columns represent the four quarters of expense data. Within each group, three colors represent the three expense categories, which are identified in the legend by the three labels from column A of the selected range: Selling Expenses, Marketing Expenses, and Overhead.

The Chart toolbar → 8. Take a couple of minutes to check out the ToolTips descriptions of the buttons on the Chart toolbar before we move on.

Sizing and Moving Charts

As we mentioned, you don't have to worry about the precise size and location of your chart when you create it, because you can always adjust the chart by dragging the small black squares, called *handles*, around the chart's frame. Try this:

← Handles

1. Point to the handle in the middle of the left side of the frame and drag it toward the center. Excel redraws the chart within a narrower frame.

2. Drag a corner handle diagonally inward to decrease both the height and the width proportionally.

3. Move the small chart by pointing anywhere inside its frame and dragging in the direction in which you want to move.

4. When you've finished experimenting, reshape the chart so that it occupies almost the entire window.

Updating Charts

Excel has actively linked your chart to its underlying data, so if you change the data, Excel automatically redraws the chart to reflect the change. Try this:

1. Scroll upward, select cell E4 on the worksheet, and reenter the 4th Quarter sales as *123456.78*. The formulas go to work, producing drastic changes in the expenses and net income.

2. Use the scroll bar to bring the modified chart into view:

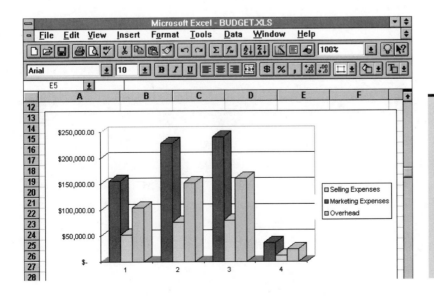

Chart scale

If you change the source data radically, the scale of the entire chart might change. For example, if you enter a sales amount in the millions in BUDGET.XLS, the other columns shrink down to almost nothing to keep the scale consistent.

3. Click the Undo button to restore the original 4th Quarter amount.

Changing the Chart Type

Now that we've covered the basics of chart building, let's plot a new chart from the quarterly sales data so that we can explore the many charting possibilities available in Excel. We will start by deleting this chart and creating a new one:

Deleting charts

1. Click the expenses chart to select it and press the Delete key. Excel removes the chart from the worksheet.

2. Press Ctrl+Home and select A3:E4. The first row in this range contains labels that identify the four quarters of the budget year, and the second row contains numeric sales data.

Creating a default chart

3. Click the ChartWizard button and drag a marquee below the budget data. Click Finish to accept all the default settings in the five ChartWizard dialog boxes. Excel draws the chart shown here:

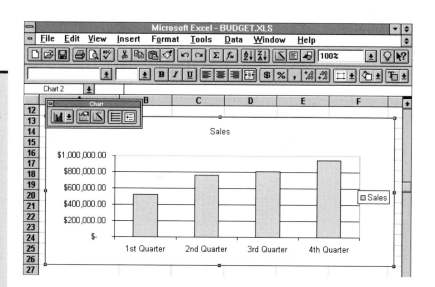

The default chart format

Initially, Excel creates charts in its default format—a plain column chart. To change the default format to the format of the active chart, choose the Options command from the Tools menu and click the Chart tab. In the Default Chart Format section, click Use The Current Chart, assign the chart format a name in the Add Custom AutoFormat dialog box, and click OK. The new name then appears in the Default Chart Format box. Click OK again. Any new chart you create will then be in this format. The new default format remains in effect until you change it.

No matter what type of chart you need—bar, pie, line, and so on—Excel has a format that will probably do the job. You can always come up with impressive visual support for a worksheet by carefully selecting from among Excel's many predefined chart types. When a chart is active, you can change the chart type by clicking the down arrow to the right of the

Chart Type button and then clicking a chart button. The available types include:

- Column charts (the default format), which are ideal for showing the variations in the value of an item over time, as with the budget example. In addition to the simple column chart that you've already seen, you can also create stacked or 100 percent stacked column charts. ← **Column charts**

- Bar charts, which are ideal for showing the variations in the value of an item over time, or for showing the values of several items at a single point in time. ← **Bar charts**

- Line charts, which are often used to show variations in the value of more than one item over time. ← **Line charts**

- Area charts, which look something like line charts but which plot multiple data series as cumulative layers with different colors, patterns, or shades. ← **Area charts**

- Pie charts, which are ideal for showing the percentages of an item that can be assigned to the item's components. (Pie charts can represent only one data range.) ← **Pie charts**

- Doughnut charts, which display the data in a doughnut shape. Similar to the pie chart, they can, however, display more than one data series. ← **Doughnut charts**

- XY (or scatter) charts, which are used to detect correlations between independent items (such as a person's height and weight). ← **XY charts**

- Radar charts, which plot each series on its own axes radiating from a center point. ← **Radar charts**

- High-low-close charts, which are typically used to plot stock-market activity. ← **High-low-close charts**

  In addition, you can create three-dimensional area, bar, column, line, pie, and surface charts. And you can create various kinds of combination charts, which plot one type of chart on top of another as an "overlay." ← **3-D charts** ← **Combination charts**

  Each gallery offers several variations that will satisfy most of your charting needs. Let's try changing the type of the chart currently on your screen so that you can see some of the possibilities:

1. With the chart selected, click the down arrow to the right of the Chart Type button on the Chart toolbar. Then click the Pie-Chart button in the left column. Excel draws a chart in which the four quarters of sales data are represented as colored wedges in a circular pie:

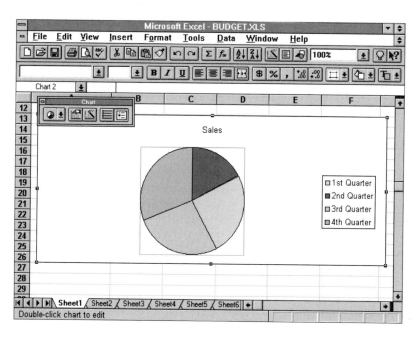

2. Click the Default Chart button to restore the previous type.

Before taking a look at some of the other types, let's add another set of data—the net income amounts—to the chart, like this:

Adding data to a chart

1. Click the worksheet, move to the budget, select A11:E11, and click the Copy button.

2. Click the chart and choose Paste Special from the Edit menu to display this dialog box:

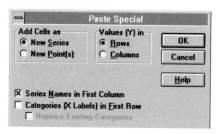

3. The default settings are correct, so click OK. Excel adds a
second series of column markers to the chart, as shown here:

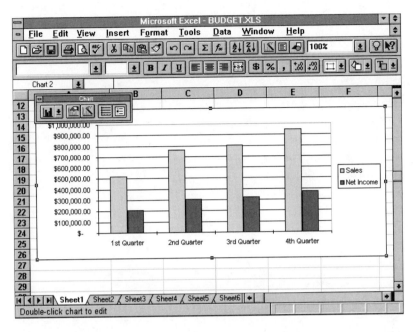

You can now compare sales with after-expenses income for
each of the four quarters. Let's see what this data looks like
in some other chart types:

1. Display the Chart Type button's list and click the Line-Chart
button. Sales and net income are now represented as two
separate lines on the chart:

Creating line charts

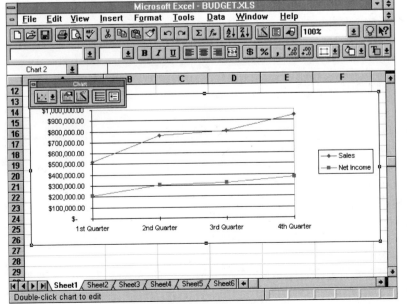

Adding values to an existing series

If you add values to a set of data
in your worksheet and want to
update a chart you created earlier
to reflect the new values, you can
select the values and simply drag
the selection to the chart. When
you release the mouse button,
Excel adds the additional data
points along the category axis.

Creating 3-D pie charts

2. Display the Chart Type button's list and click the 3D-Pie-Chart button. Now the four quarters of sales data are represented as colored wedges in a circular pie with the illusion of three dimensions. You no longer see the net income data because a pie chart can display only one set of data.

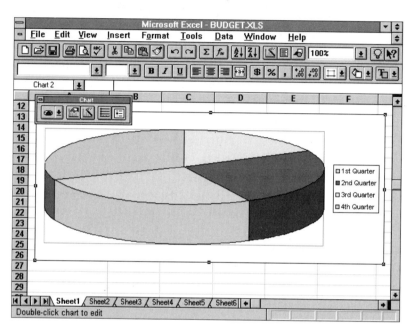

Creating doughnut charts

3. Finally, click the Doughnut-Chart button in the Chart Type button's list. The resulting chart displays two circles, one for each type of data:

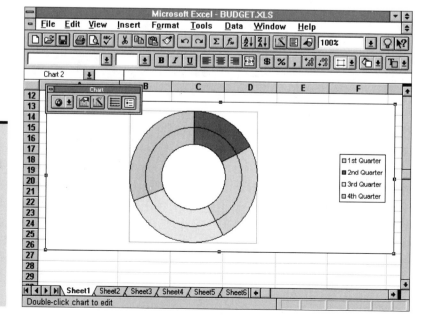

X-axis and y-axis

Excel uses the terms *x-axis* and *y-axis* with some of its chart commands. For clarification, here are a couple of definitions: The x-axis shows the information categories—for example, sales and expenses; the y-axis shows the data points (plotted values).

4. Click the other chart buttons to get an idea of what's available. Finish up with a simple two-dimensional column chart.

Using Chart Autoformats

Often, clicking one of the options in the Chart Type button's list will produce exactly the chart you need, but sometimes you might want something slightly different. Before you spend time adjusting the format of a chart type, you should explore Excel's *chart autoformats*. These subtypes are displayed when you choose the AutoFormat command from the Format menu. Follow these steps:

Chart autoformats

1. Double-click anywhere within the chart. If your chart fits within the worksheet window, Excel surrounds the chart with a shaded border. If the chart's frame stretches beyond the edges of the worksheet window, Excel opens the chart in its own window. Either way, Excel changes the menus on the menu bar to accommodate the commands appropriate for working with charts.

2. Choose AutoFormat from the Format menu to display this dialog box:

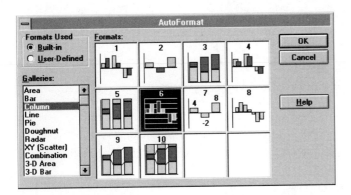

Because the active chart is a column chart, Column is selected as the chart type in the Galleries list, and the default column autoformat, number 6, is highlighted in the Formats section.

3. Select 3-D Bar from the Galleries list to display the gallery of 3-D bar autoformats shown on the next page.

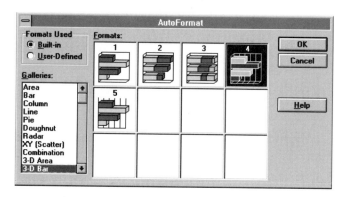

4. Click format number 5 and then click OK. Here is the result:

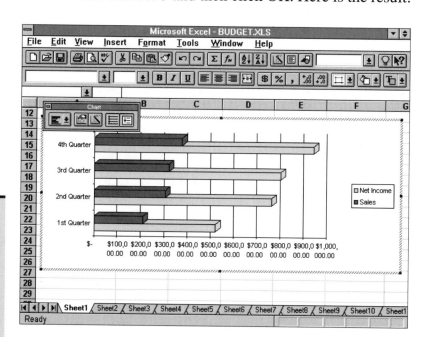

Combination charts

To create a combination chart, select Combination from the Galleries list in the AutoFormat dialog box and then select one of the autoformats. You can plot your data as one chart type overlaid by another chart type—for example, a column chart overlaid by a line chart. If your data includes series that span widely divergent ranges of values, you can plot the data against two y-axes of different scales—for example, one series against a y-axis on the left of the chart ranging from 0 to 100 and another series on the right of the chart ranging from 100,000 to 1,000,000.

You might want to explore some of the other available chart autoformats. In particular, try creating a combination chart.

Customizing Charts

As we have said, Excel has a chart type for almost every occasion. But often you will want to refine the presentation of a chart by adding or changing specific elements. For this purpose, Excel provides a wealth of options you can use to customize your charts. We'll review some of these options and make changes to the chart by adding titles, adding a frame, and changing grid lines. These elements increase almost any chart's clarity and persuasiveness.

Shortcut menus exist for almost every conceivable chart element. You might want to get a feel for the range of customization possibilities by right-clicking various chart elements (grid lines, axes, series, and so on) to open their shortcut menus. When you've finished experimenting on your own, we'll show you how to add a title to the chart currently on your screen.

Adding and Formatting Text

To dress up the chart, you can add a title with a subtitle and explanatory notes. (Titles appear at the top of the chart; notes can be placed anywhere on the chart.) You can also customize the axis labels. All the fonts and attributes available for worksheet entries are available for chart text, so you can format the text any way you want. Follow these steps to add your own title to the chart:

1. With the chart selected, right-click in the area above the legend and choose Insert Titles from the shortcut menu to display this dialog box:

Adding a chart title

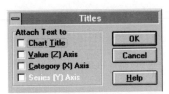

As you can see from the options, you can create a title and attach text to either axis.

2. Click Chart Title and then click OK. Excel places the word *Title* in a frame above the chart.

3. Select the word *Title*, type *1994 Budget*, press Enter, and type *Sales and Net Income*. Then click anywhere on the chart to complete entry of the title, which now looks as shown on the next page.

Adding notes

To add explanatory notes to a chart, check that no chart element is selected, click an insertion point in the formula bar, type the note, and press Enter. Excel displays a text box containing the note in the middle of the chart. You can use the handles around the text box to reposition it or resize it. To format the text box and the note it contains, right-click the box and make your selections on the tabs of the Format Text Box dialog box.

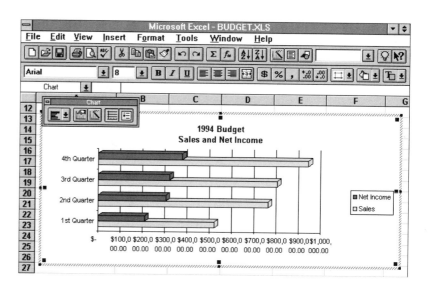

Formatting the title

4. Right-click *1994 Budget* to display the title's shortcut menu. Then choose Format Chart Title and click the Font tab:

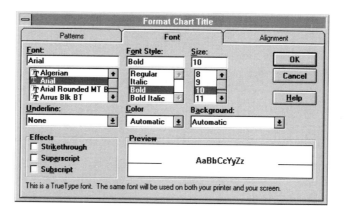

Creating graphics in Excel

With Excel's drawing tools, located on the Drawing toolbar (see page 154), you can draw attention to specific parts of your chart. For example, you might circle a data point or mark it with an arrow. You can even create simple graphics, such as a logo. The best way to learn how to use the Line, Rectangle, Oval, and Arc buttons is to experiment. To create a graphic object, click one of the buttons and drag it over the worksheet. Holding down the Shift key as you drag constrains lines to 45-degree angles and creates perfect squares, circles, and arcs. When you release the mouse button, Excel surrounds the object with handles that you can use to reposition and resize the object. Choose the Object command from the Format menu to adjust the object's line thickness, fill color, and pattern. To manipulate several objects as a group, click the Selection button, drag a box around the objects to select them, and then click the Group button. Click the Bring To Front and Send To Back buttons to adjust the order of objects stacked on top of one another. Click the Text Box button to add free-floating notes to a worksheet.

5. Select Times New Roman from the Font list, click Bold Italic in the Font Style list, and click OK.

Now let's make the default value-axis labels easier to read:

1. Right-click the value-axis numbers, choose Format Axis from the shortcut menu, and click the Number tab:

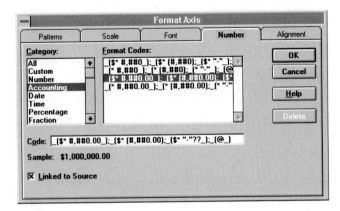

2. Select the Currency category and then click the Scale tab to accept the default selection in the Format Code list and display these Scale tab options:

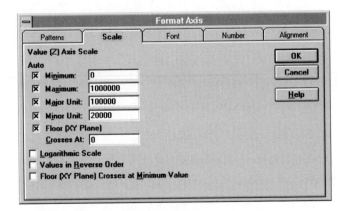

3. Under Auto, you can see that the value axis is scaled from 0 to 1 million, with a label at major-unit intervals of 100,000. Double-click the Major Unit edit box and type *2000000* to display half as many labels along the value axis. Then click OK to see the results shown on the next page.

Formatting legends

By default, Excel places the legend to the right of the plot area. If you want, you can move the legend to another part of the screen by simply dragging it. Alternatively, you can choose Format Legend from the legend's shortcut menu and select an option on the Placement tab in the Format Legend dialog box. Other tabs in this dialog box allow you to change the pattern, color, and font of the legend.

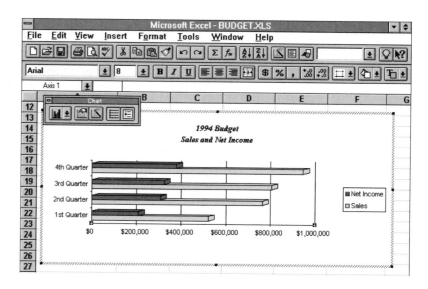

Enhancing the Chart's Border

The Color and Font Color buttons on the Formatting toolbar allow you to select colors and patterns for different elements of your chart and your worksheets. However, using the Format command on the shortcut menu is the quickest way to customize the chart's border. Here's how:

1. Right-click the background of the chart near the outer border and choose Format Chart Area from the shortcut menu to display this dialog box:

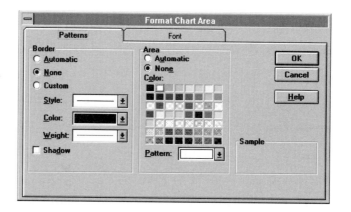

Formatting data markers

To change the color, pattern, or the legend name for a series of data markers, right-click one of the markers and choose Format Data Series from the shortcut menu. Excel displays a dialog box in which you can make these and other types of changes to the markers.

2. Click the down arrow to the right of the Weight edit box in the Border section and select the third line. Click the Shadow box and then click OK.

You can also use this dialog box to give the chart's background a color or pattern.

Adding Grid Lines

When grid lines would make it easier to read the plotted data, you can easily add them to your charts. You can add lines for major or minor intervals on either or both axes. Our chart has grid lines for the value axis showing the dollar amounts. Let's add grid lines to the category axis:

1. Right-click a blank area between the existing grid lines and choose Insert Gridlines from the shortcut menu to display this dialog box:

2. Click Major Gridlines in the Category [X] Axis section and then click OK. The chart now looks like this:

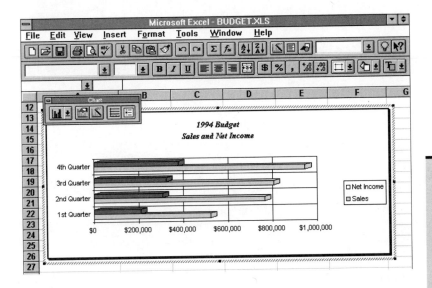

3. Click twice anywhere on the worksheet to deselect the chart and remove the Chart toolbar. (If the chart is displayed in its own window, double-click the Control menu icon at the left

The SERIES function

If you click one of the columns in the chart, a SERIES function appears in the formula bar. This function links the chart to the source worksheet. Notice that the references are all absolute. If you change the position of the charted data in the source worksheet, Excel will not be able to find the moved data.

end of the window's title bar.) Then save the workbook before moving on.

We won't take our customization experiments any further but will leave you to explore on your own. When you're ready, rejoin us to print your chart.

Previewing and Printing Charts

Previewing and printing charts is much like previewing and printing worksheets. You can preview and print the worksheet data and chart together or just the chart. Follow these steps:

Bird's-eye view

1. Press Ctrl+Home, and then click the Print Preview button. Your screen now looks like this one:

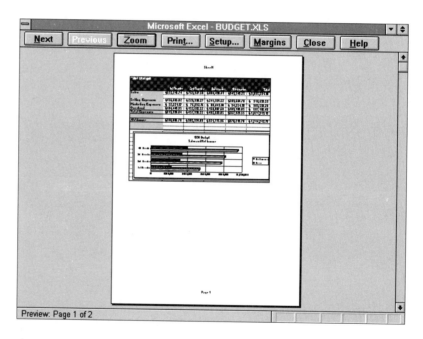

As you can see, one or two adjustments would greatly improve the look of this page.

2. Click the Close button to return to the worksheet. Then adjust the position and size of the chart so that it is centered on columns A through F and separated from the worksheet entries by about five rows of blank cells.

3. Click the Print Preview button again, and then click the Setup button on the Print Preview toolbar.

4. Click the Margins tab, change the Top margin to *1.5*, and in the Center On Page section, select the Horizontally option.

5. Click the Header/Footer tab, click the down arrow to the right of the Header option, and select (none) from the top of the drop-down list. Repeat this step for the Footer option.

6. Click the Sheet tab, click the Gridlines option to deselect it, and click OK. Here are the results:

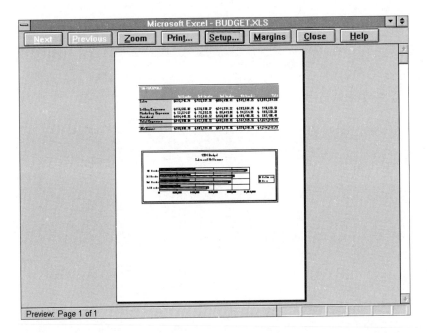

If you want, you can now click the Print button to create a paper copy of your chart.

Excel's charting features make creating charts easy, and with the shortcut menus, adding special touches is a snap. Be creative and have fun!

5

Multiple Worksheets and Scenarios

What you will learn...

Calculate basic salary information

EMPLOYEE INFORMATION

Name	Salary	Salary/Hour	Emp. Costs	Costs/Hour	Hourly Rate	Billable
Baker, Susan	32,000	21.33	7,040	4.51	26	y
Cash, John	22,000	14.67	4,840	3.10	18	y
Collins, Peter	40,000	26.67	8,800	5.64	32	y
Dixon, Sally	50,000	33.33	11,000	7.05	40	
Marsh, Robin	27,000	18.00	5,940	3.81	22	y
Maxwell, Mary	18,000	12.00	3,960	2.54	15	y
Parkins, Dee						
Sanders, Ann						
Sexton, Alex						
West, Toby						

Calculate basic overhead

OVERHEAD (FIXED) COSTS

Name	Salary	Salary/Hour	Emp. Costs	Costs/Hour	Hourly Rate
Dixon, Sally	50,000	33.33	11,000	7.05	40
Parkins, Dee	22,000	14.67	4,840	3.10	18

Expenses	Budget
Rent	24,000
Insurance	
Equipment	
Supplies	
Total	

Resolve circular references with iteration

PROJECT COST ESTIMATE

Date	Personnel Cost $ 7,368.00
Client	Direct Expenses $ 710.00
Project	Total Cost $ 8,078.00
Estimate $ 12,427.69	Profit Margin $ 4,349.69

Name	Hours	Hourly Rate	Billable Rate	Billable Total
Baker, Susan	48	$ 26.00	$ 37.00	$ 1,776.00
Marsh, Robin	80	$ 22.00	$ 33.00	$ 2,640.00
Maxwell, Mary	40	$ 15.00	$ 26.00	$ 1,040.00
Sanders, Ann	40	$ 16.00	$ 27.00	$ 1,080.00
West, Toby	32	$ 15.00	$ 26.00	$ 832.00

Scenario Summary

	Current Values:	Current Location	First Location	Second Location
Changing Cells:				
$B$9	24,000	24,000	32,000	37,000
$B$10	1,350	1,350	2,100	3,100
$B$11	10,000	10,000	12,500	17,000
$B$12	7,000	7,000	8,000	10,000
Result Cells:				
OVER_RATE	11	11	12	13

Notes: Current Values column represents values of changing cells at time Scenario Summary Report was created. Changing cells for each scenario are highlighted in gray.

Create scenarios to evaluate the effect of changes

Look up information in other workbooks

In this chapter, we tackle a more ambitious set of work-sheets. First we create tables of employee information and overhead costs. Then we create a worksheet in another workbook that estimates project costs by "looking up" hourly rates in one of the tables. Next, we cover a technique called *iteration*, which enables Excel to resolve circular calculations. Finally, we use Excel's Scenario Manager to create multiple versions, or scenarios, of our cost sheet to reflect different situations.

Deciding what information you'll need

In our example, we create only employee information and overhead tables, because the primary cost involved in the sample project estimate is for people's time. However, you can easily adapt the project cost-estimate worksheet to incorporate marketing expenses or materials information. For example, if you manage a construction business that specializes in bathroom and kitchen remodeling, you can create a table with up-to-date prices for fixtures, plumbing supplies, cabinets, tile, and so on, in addition to the employee information and overhead tables. Even if you are a one-person operation with no employees, you can still adapt the worksheet to make sure that you include overhead and marketing costs in your project estimates.

This chapter differs from previous chapters in that we don't bog down the instructions with information you already know. For example, we might show you a worksheet and ask you to create it, without always telling you step by step what to enter, how to apply formats and styles, and how to adjust column widths. We leave it up to you to create the worksheet using the illustration as a guide. Similarly, we might tell you to create a formula, assuming that you know how to enter a function in a cell and how to click cells to use their references as arguments.

For this example, we'll organize the project information in two sheets, Employee and Overhead, saved within a single workbook. We'll also work with two different workbooks and show you how to create links between them.

Creating the Supporting Tables

The logical way to begin this example is to enter the data needed for the two supporting tables. There's nothing complicated about these tables; we've stripped them down so that you don't have to type any extraneous information. The few calculations involved have been greatly simplified and do not reflect the gyrations accountants would go through to ensure to-the-penny accuracy. So instead of describing step by step how to create these tables, we'll simply show them to you and, after discussing the few formulas and cell and range names involved, let you create them on your own.

1. Open a new workbook, rename Sheet1 as Employee, and then save the workbook in the EXCEL\EXAMPLES directory as COSTS.XLS.

The Employee sheet

2. Create the following table of employee information:

	Name	Salary	Salary/Hour	Emp. Costs	Costs/Hour	Hourly Rate	Billable
4	Baker, Susan	32000					y
5	Cash, John	22000					y
6	Collins, Peter	40000					y
7	Dixon, Sally	50000					
8	Marsh, Robin	27000					y
9	Maxwell, Mary	18000					y
10	Parkins, Dee	22000					
11	Sanders, Ann	20000					y
12	Sexton, Alex	24000					y
13	West, Toby	19000					y

3. In row 4, enter these formulas:

C4   =B4/50/30
Annual salary divided by 50 weeks (allowing 2 weeks for vacation), divided by 30 billable hours per week (allowing 2 hours per day of non-billable time)

Ascending order

You can list employees in the employee information table in any order, but before Excel can use the table to look up information, you must sort it in ascending order. Excel cannot look up information in randomly ordered tables or in tables in descending order. Select the range and use the Sort command on the Data menu to sort the table.

D4	=B4*.22
	Employer contributions to social security and benefits estimated at 22 percent of annual salary
E4	=D4/52/30
	Employer contributions to social security and benefits divided by 52 weeks divided by 30 hours per week
The ROUND function → F4	=ROUND(C4+E4,0)
	Salary per hour plus benefits per hour, rounded to a whole number (0 decimal places)

4. After entering the formulas in row 4, select C4:F13 and choose Fill and then Down from the Edit menu to copy the row 4 formulas to rows 5 through 13.

5. Use the Comma Style and Decrease Decimal buttons on the Formatting toolbar to add commas and display no decimals in the amounts in columns B and D. Use the Decrease Decimal button to display two decimals in the amounts in columns C and E. Then adjust the column widths as needed to make the table more readable.

6. Choose Name and then Define from the Insert menu to assign the name BILLABLE to cells G4:G14 and the name EMP_RATE to cells A4:F14. (See page 41 for information about how to assign range names.) We'll use these names in future formulas to create links between this and other worksheets. Press Ctrl+Home and save your work. Here is the completed table:

Extending named ranges

It is a good idea to include a blank row or column at the end of the range when assigning range names. If you need to add employees to the Employee sheet, for example, you can then select the blank row below the last entry and choose Insert from the Edit menu to add a new row. Because the blank row is part of the range named BILLABLE, Excel automatically extends the range name definition to include the new row.

Microsoft Excel - COSTS.XLS

File Edit View Insert Format Tools Data Window Help

Arial   10   B I U

	A	B	C	D	E	F	G
1		EMPLOYEE INFORMATION					
2							
3	Name	Salary	Salary/Hour	Emp. Costs	Costs/Hour	Hourly Rate	Billable
4	Baker, Susan	32,000	21.33	7,040	4.51	26	y
5	Cash, John	22,000	14.67	4,840	3.10	18	y
6	Collins, Peter	40,000	26.67	8,800	5.64	32	y
7	Dixon, Sally	50,000	33.33	11,000	7.05	40	
8	Marsh, Robin	27,000	18.00	5,940	3.81	22	y
9	Maxwell, Mary	18,000	12.00	3,960	2.54	15	y
10	Parkins, Dee	22,000	14.67	4,840	3.10	18	
11	Sanders, Ann	20,000	13.33	4,400	2.82	16	y
12	Sexton, Alex	24,000	16.00	5,280	3.38	19	y
13	West, Toby	19,000	12.67	4,180	2.68	15	y
14							
15							

That's it for the employee information table. Let's move on to the overhead table:

1. Click Sheet2 to move to a new sheet and rename the sheet as Overhead. Then create the first part of the table shown here:

The Overhead sheet

	Microsoft Excel - COSTS.XLS						
File Edit View Insert Format Tools Data Window Help							

	A	B	C	D	E	F	G
1		OVERHEAD (FIXED) COSTS					
2							
3	Name	Salary	Salary/Hour	Emp. Costs	Costs/Hour	Hourly Rate	
4	Dixon, Sally	50,000					
5	Parkins, Dee	22,000					
6							
7							
8	Expenses	Budget					
9	Rent	24,000					
10	Insurance	1,350					
11	Equipment	10,000					
12	Supplies	7,000					
13							
14	Total						

2. Sally Dixon and Dee Parkins are administrative employees who do not directly generate income for the company, so we need to include their salaries and benefits in this overhead calculation. You can copy the entries from row 4 of the Employee sheet using the Copy and Paste buttons, or you can enter them from scratch. If you choose to enter them from scratch, here are the formulas to use in row 4:

C4	=B4/50/30 (with 2-decimal format)
D4	=B4*.22 (with Comma 0-decimal format)
E4	=D4/52/30 (with 2-decimal format)
F4	=ROUND(C4+E4,0) (with 0-decimal format)

3. After completing the formulas in row 4, copy them to row 5.

4. Next, enter *Expenses/Hour* in cell E14 and *Total Billable Overhead/Hour* in cell E16. Select both entries and click the Bold and Align Right buttons. The worksheet looks like the one on the next page.

Making entries in multiple sheets

When building two or more worksheets with similar layouts, you can select the sheets to form a group and build the layout on all the sheets at the same time. Select multiple sheets by holding down the Shift key and clicking their sheet tabs. Select consecutive sheets by displaying the first sheet and clicking the tab of the last sheet. The word *Group* appears in the title bar and the selected sheet tabs turn white. You can then build the worksheet. Whatever you do on the displayed worksheet is also applied to the other members of the group. When you finish, ungroup the sheets by choosing Ungroup Sheets from the shortcut menu.

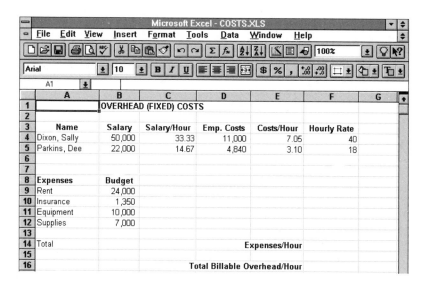

5. Now enter and format these formulas in the designated cells:

B14	=SUM(B9:B13)
F14	=ROUND(B14/52/30,0)
F16	=SUM(F4:F14)

You must bill 30 hours each week at the rate in F16 to cover overhead costs. You cannot bill overhead to a client directly, so you must increase the hourly rate of employees with billable hours by a prorated amount to ensure that overhead is included in project estimates. To calculate the prorated overhead amount, you need to divide the total billable rate per hour in cell F16 by the number of employees who generate income. You can glance at the Employee sheet and know that this number is 8, but what if the company had many employees? You need to reference the cells in the Billable column of the Employee sheet so that Excel can supply this number.

Counting Entries

COUNTA vs. COUNT

Don't confuse the COUNTA function with the COUNT function. COUNTA tells you how many cells in the selected range contain entries of any sort, whereas COUNT tells you how many cells in the range contain numeric values.

You can tell Excel to count the number of employees who have a *y* entry in the Billable column of the Employee sheet by using the COUNTA function. This function scans the range specified as its argument and counts the number of nonblank cells in the range. Here's how to use COUNTA in the formula that calculates the overhead allocation:

1. In cell E17 in the Overhead sheet, type *Prorated Overhead/Hour* and click the Confirm button.

2. Format the cell by clicking the Bold and Align Right buttons.

3. You want the prorated amount to be in whole dollars, so you need to nest the prorated calculation in a ROUND function. In cell F17, type the following:

=ROUND(F16/COUNTA(

To divide the hourly overhead in cell F16 by the number of employees whose hours are billable, press F3 to display the Paste Name dialog box:

Pasting a name into
a function

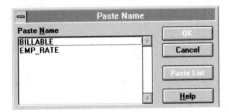

Select Billable and click OK. Type *)* to close the COUNTA function and then type *,0)* to close the ROUND function. Check that the following function is in the formula bar:

=ROUND(F16/COUNTA(BILLABLE),0)

Then click the Confirm button. Excel calculates the formula and enters the value 11 in cell F17, as shown here:

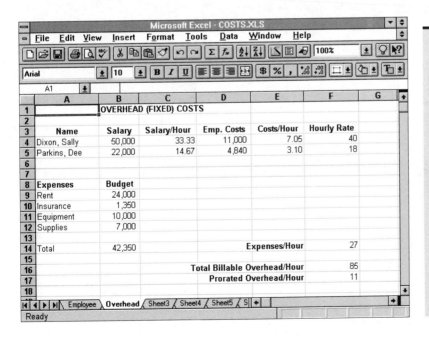

Listing names

Excel keeps track of the ranges to which you have applied a name. You can click a cell in a worksheet, press F3 to display the Paste Name dialog box, and then click the Paste List button to insert a list of range names with their references in the worksheet, starting at the selected cell. If you often assign names (and especially if you use multiple sheets within a workbook), this list can be useful in tracking the locations of the names in the workbook.

4. Assign the name OVER_RATE to cell F17, and save the workbook by clicking the Save button.

Creating the Estimate Worksheet

With the two tables in place, we're ready to create the worksheet for estimating project costs. We'll build this worksheet in a new workbook. Let's take a few moments to discuss this workbook concept. With the introduction of workbooks comes a new way of handling worksheets. The purpose of workbooks is to be able to store related sheets of information in one book. For example, if you invoice clients using worksheets, you may want to create a workbook for each client that contains a sheet for each invoice. Or if you don't need to keep an electronic version of every invoice, you could set up a workbook called INVOICES that contains a reusable invoice sheet for each client. With a little forethought, you can take advantage of the workbook concept to add a new dimension to your worksheet organization.

In the example we use here, we store the Employee and Overhead sheets in one workbook and then create another workbook for project estimates that uses a new sheet for each project. The employee and overhead information is not stored in the project estimate workbook because it is essential business information that might be needed in other types of calculations. By isolating information of this type in its own workbook, you ensure that you don't have to go hunting for it each time you need it.

Now let's open a new workbook and build the basic structure of the project cost-estimate worksheet. Then we'll fill in the formulas necessary for the calculations.

1. Click the New Workbook button on the Standard toolbar and save the new workbook in the EXCEL\EXAMPLES directory as ESTIMATE.XLS. Then create the top area of the worksheet, as shown here:

Workbooks as organizing tools

Flexible formulas

Keep in mind that using names in formulas makes your worksheets much more flexible than using cell references. If the information referenced in a formula moves because of changes you make to a worksheet, Excel adjusts the definition of the name so that the formula continues to access the correct information.

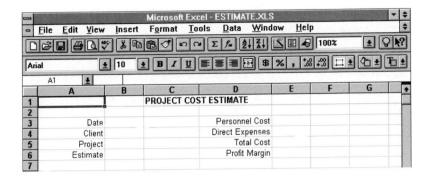

2. Next, enter the headings in row 9 for the table where you'll calculate the personnel costs of the project and enter the employee names and the number of hours you anticipate each will need to work on this project, as shown here:

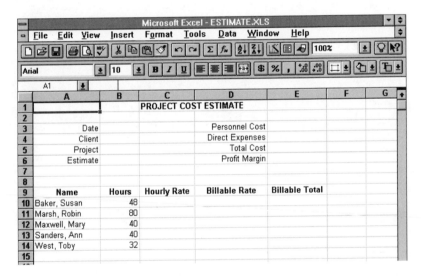

So far, everything has been pretty straightforward and has provided you with nothing more challenging than an opportunity to practice skills you learned in other chapters. Now we need to introduce the Excel function that will enable you to use one of the tables you created earlier to fill in the information needed for this worksheet.

Looking Up Information

Excel has a variety of functions you can use in formulas to look up information in worksheet tables. Among them are VLOOKUP (which is for vertically oriented tables), and HLOOKUP (which is for horizontally oriented tables). In this section, we'll show you how to use VLOOKUP.

Functions for looking up information

The VLOOKUP function ───────►

Excel needs three pieces of information to carry out the VLOOKUP function: the entry you want it to look up, the range of the lookup table, and the column number in the table from which the function should copy a value. To search for a value in the lookup table, you supply these three pieces of information in this way:

=VLOOKUP(*lookup_value,table,column_index*)

Excel searches down the leftmost column of the lookup table for the row that contains the value you supply as the first argument. Then, if Excel finds the value, the VLOOKUP function returns the value from the intersection of the same row and the column you supply as the third argument. For example, to look up the hourly rate for John Cash in the employee information table, you could move to the Employee sheet and enter the following function—say, in cell A17:

=VLOOKUP("Cash, John",A4:G13,6)

Excel scans the leftmost column of the table in A4:G13—column A—for the lookup value *Cash, John*. When it finds the value it's looking for in cell A5, it looks across the same row to the sixth column—column F—and copies the value 18 from cell F5 to cell A17.

Let's see how to put the VLOOKUP function to work:

1. In Sheet1 of the ESTIMATE workbook, select cell C10 and click the Function Wizard button. With the Most Recently Used option selected in the Function Category list, select VLOOKUP from the Function Name list and click the Next button to display this dialog box:

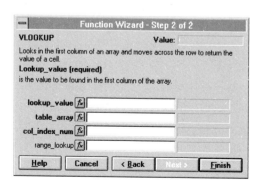

2. With the insertion point in the *lookup_value* edit box, click cell A10 on the worksheet. The Function Wizard enters A10 in the edit box and displays the contents of the cell in the adjacent box.

Specifying the lookup value

3. Click the *table_array* edit box and choose COSTS.XLS from the bottom of the Window menu. Click the Employee tab to display that sheet, click the down arrow to the right of the Name box, and then select EMP_RATE. The Function Wizard enters a reference to the selected workbook and sheet in the *table_array* edit box and establishes a "link" between the ESTIMATE and COSTS workbooks by using the name of the COSTS workbook in the formula it is building in the formula bar.

Specifying the lookup table

4. Click the *col_index_num* edit box and type *6* to tell Excel to find the answer in the sixth column.

Specifying the lookup column

5. Click the Finish button. Excel immediately looks up the value in cell A10 (Baker, Susan) in the table named EMP_RATE in COSTS.XLS and enters the corresponding hourly rate in cell C10 of ESTIMATE.XLS, as shown here:

	A	B	C	D	E	F	G
1			PROJECT COST ESTIMATE				
2							
3	Date			Personnel Cost			
4	Client			Direct Expenses			
5	Project			Total Cost			
6	Estimate			Profit Margin			
7							
8							
9	Name	Hours	Hourly Rate	Billable Rate	Billable Total		
10	Baker, Susan	48	26				
11	Marsh, Robin	80					
12	Maxwell, Mary	40					
13	Sanders, Ann	40					
14	West, Toby	32					

6. Now all you have to do is use AutoFill to copy the formula in cell C10 to C11:C14. Then equivalent formulas will look up the hourly rates for the other people who will be involved in this project.

Easy opening of linked worksheets

When a worksheet contains a reference to a cell on a sheet in a different workbook, Excel retrieves the contents of the "external" cell every time you open the worksheet. The external workbook doesn't have to be open for this retrieval to take place, but if you want, you can easily open it by choosing the Links command from the Edit menu. Excel displays a dialog box listing all workbooks that are referred to by formulas in the active worksheet. Select the workbook you want to open and click the Open button.

Completing the Estimate

Well, the hard part is over. A few simple calculations, and you'll be ready to prepare an estimate for your client.

1. In the ESTIMATE workbook, enter the following formula:

   D10   =C10+COSTS.XLS!OVER_RATE

   (You can use the Window menu to select the COSTS workbook. Then click the Overhead tab and select the range name from the name box's drop-down list. Press Enter to place the formula in the cell and return to the ESTIMATE workbook.)

2. Enter this formula in the indicated cell:

   E10   =B10*D10

3. Use AutoFill to copy the formulas to D11:E14.

4. Select C10:E14 and click the Currency Style button on the Formatting toolbar.

5. Now add lines to your table. Select A9:E9, click the Border button's down arrow, and click the third button in the second row. Then select A14:E14, click the Border button's down arrow, and click the second button in the first row.

6. Press Ctrl+Home to view the results:

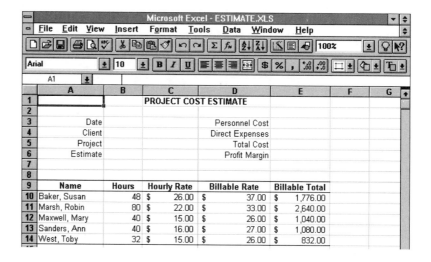

Now you can calculate total costs in the summary area at the top of the worksheet:

1. Make these entries in the indicated cells:

E3	=SUM(E10:E14)
E4	710
E5	=E3+E4

2. Use the Currency Style button to format cell E4. The entry in this cell is an estimate of charges that will be incurred for long-distance phone calls, delivery services, and other expenses attributable directly to the project. As you can see, this worksheet is almost complete:

	A	B	C	D	E
1			PROJECT COST ESTIMATE		
2					
3	Date			Personnel Cost	$ 7,368.00
4	Client			Direct Expenses	$ 710.00
5	Project			Total Cost	$ 8,078.00
6	Estimate			Profit Margin	
7					
8					
9	Name	Hours	Hourly Rate	Billable Rate	Billable Total
10	Baker, Susan	48	$ 26.00	$ 37.00	$ 1,776.00
11	Marsh, Robin	80	$ 22.00	$ 33.00	$ 2,640.00
12	Maxwell, Mary	40	$ 15.00	$ 26.00	$ 1,040.00
13	Sanders, Ann	40	$ 16.00	$ 27.00	$ 1,080.00
14	West, Toby	32	$ 15.00	$ 26.00	$ 832.00

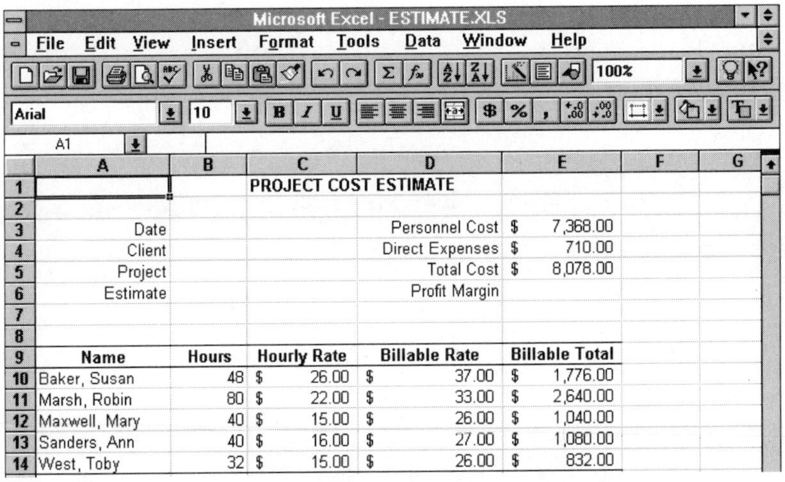

Projecting Profit Margin with Iteration

Probably the most difficult part of estimating a project is figuring out the profit margin. You now have a good idea what this project is going to cost. But suppose you need a margin of roughly 35 percent of the estimate total to be sure you make a profit. How do you calculate the actual profit margin when you don't yet know the estimate total, and how do you calculate the estimate total when you don't know the profit margin? You could go in circles forever.

Circular references

Fortunately, you can have Excel go in circles for you. Using the iteration technique, you can force Excel to calculate the margin formula over and over until it can give you an answer. Follow the steps on the next page.

1. Select cell E6 in the ESTIMATE workbook, click the Currency Style button, and enter this formula:

   =.35*B6

2. Now select cell B6, click the Currency Style button, and enter this formula:

   =SUM(E5:E6)

   When you enter the second formula, Excel displays a message box stating that it cannot resolve circular references.

3. Click OK to close the message box. The message *Circular:E6* appears in the status bar, telling you that the formula in E6 is the culprit.

What is a circular reference?

This formula multiplies the sum of cells E5 and E6 (the formula in cell B6) by 35 percent. Excel cannot arrive at a result because when it adds E5 and E6, the formula in E6 must be recalculated; and as soon as Excel recalculates the formula, E6 changes, so E5 and E6 must be added again and so on, forever. Here's how to force Excel to come up with an answer:

1. Choose Options from the Tools menu and click the Calculation tab. Excel displays the options shown here:

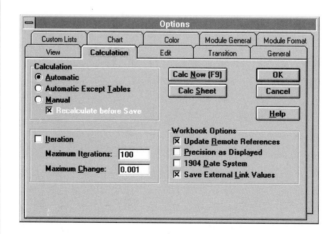

Types of calculation

By default, Excel immediately calculates a formula when you enter it and also recalculates any of the existing formulas in open worksheets that are affected by the new entry. To tell Excel to calculate open worksheets only when you press the F9 key, choose Options from the Tools menu, click the Calculation tab, and then select the Manual option. You might want to activate this option for large worksheets, where recalculating each formula can take some time.

2. Select the Iteration option, and then click OK. You return to the worksheet, where Excel quickly recalculates the formulas, finally coming up with the results shown here:

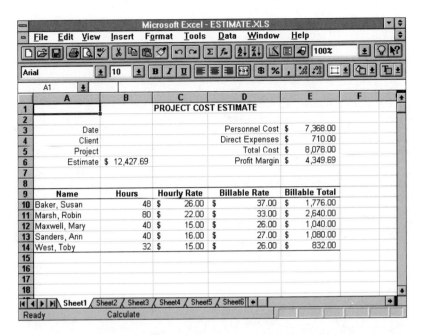

By selecting the Iteration option, you tell Excel to ignore the circular reference and to keep recalculating the formula, going in circles until it comes up with the best possible results. By default, Excel recalculates the formulas 100 times or until the values change by less than .001. The result might not be exact, but inaccuracies this minuscule are not likely to cause concern.

Working with Multiple Scenarios

The completed project estimate worksheet shows current employee and overhead costs. Suppose your company will be moving into a new facility next year and is looking at two possible locations. How will the move affect overhead costs and, therefore, project costs? You can use Excel's Scenario Manager to create multiple *scenarios* of the expense information so that you can analyze project costs before and after the move.

Scenario Manager

To demonstrate some of the capabilities of Scenario Manager, we'll assign the current nonemployee expenses of the overhead table to a scenario name and create two other scenarios for future nonemployee expenses. Then we'll change the scenarios to see the effect on project costs.

Creating Scenarios

Let's start by designating the expenses range as the changing cells in the scenarios:

1. Switch to the COSTS workbook and select the Overhead sheet. Then select B9:B12 and choose Scenarios from the Tools menu to display this Scenario Manager dialog box:

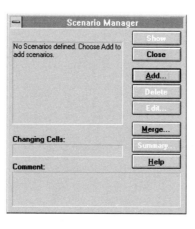

Adding the first scenario

2. Click the Add button to display this dialog box:

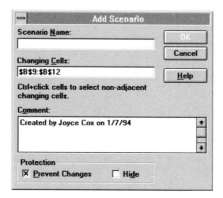

3. Excel has entered the selected range in the Changing Cells edit box. Type *Current Location* in the Scenario Name edit box and click OK to display the Scenario Values dialog box:

Merging scenarios

You can create a worksheet with a scenario and send copies to colleagues to input their scenario values. When they return their copies, you can click the Merge button in the Scenario Manager dialog box, select their worksheets, and merge them into Scenario Manager, where you can view and edit their scenarios or use them in summary reports.

4. The values displayed are those selected in the worksheet. Click Add to keep these values and add the second scenario.

Adding a second scenario

5. Type *First Location* in the Scenario Name edit box and click OK to display the Scenario Values dialog box.

6. Change the values as shown here:

1.	$B$9	32000
2.	$B$10	2100
3.	$B$11	12500
4.	$B$12	8000

Then click Add again to keep these numbers and add the third scenario.

Adding a third scenario

7. Type *Second Location* in the Scenario Name edit box and click OK.

8. Change the values as shown here:

1.	$B$9	37000
2.	$B$10	3100
3.	$B$11	17000
4.	$B$12	10000

Then click OK to return to the Scenario Manager dialog box, which now looks like this:

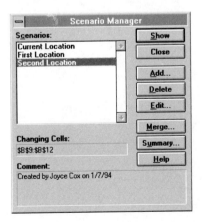

9. Click Close to return to the workbook.

Changing Scenarios

By changing scenarios, you can display different versions of a worksheet to see the results of various conditions or assumptions. In the project cost-estimate worksheet, you can use the scenarios you've created to show the effect of future facility costs on project costs and profit margin.

To make it easier to access the scenarios and see their effects, we'll display the COSTS and ESTIMATES workbooks side by side and use the Scenarios box on the WorkGroup toolbar. Follow these steps to set up your screen:

1. Choose Arrange from the Windows menu and click OK to accept the default Tiled option. Then bring columns D and E into view in the ESTIMATE.XLS window.

The Workgroup toolbar →

2. Right-click the toolbar area and choose Workgroup from the toolbar shortcut menu. Arrange the toolbar as shown here, and then use ToolTips to get an idea of what the toolbar's buttons do.

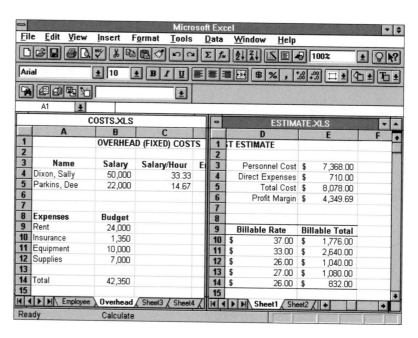

You are now ready to run the scenarios. Here's how:

1. Activate COSTS.XLS, click the down arrow to the right of the Scenarios box on the Workgroup toolbar, and select First Location. The expense cells change based on the values we defined for the First Location scenario, and Excel recalculates both workbooks, like this:

Selecting a scenario

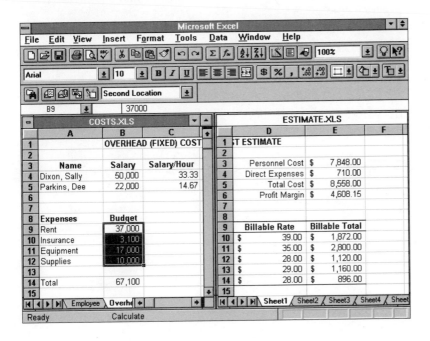

2. Now select Second Location from the Scenario drop-down list to produce these results:

3. Return the expense cells to their original values by selecting Current Location from the Scenarios drop-down list. Then click the COSTS.XLS Maximize button.

4. Remove the Workgroup toolbar by right-clicking the toolbar area and choosing Workgroup from the shortcut menu to toggle it off.

Creating Scenario Reports

The Scenario Summary →

Now that we have completed the building of the scenarios, let's use Scenario Manager to print a report. The Scenario Summary report displays the values of all the scenarios and their effects on the result cells. In this example, the result cell is the Prorated Overhead/Hour amount in cell F17 in the Overhead sheet of the COSTS workbook. It shows the amount of increase in the hourly rate of employees needed to ensure that the increase in overhead is taken into account in project estimates. Here's how to generate a report:

1. Choose Scenarios from the Tools menu to display the Scenario Manager dialog box.

2. Click the Summary button, which displays this dialog box:

By default, Scenario Manager has selected the Scenario Summary option in the Report Type section and entered an absolute reference to $F$17 in the Result Cells edit box.

3. Click OK. Scenario Manager creates a new sheet named Scenario Summary between the Employee and Overhead sheets in the COSTS workbook and builds the report.

4. Maximize the COSTS.XLS window and scroll column G into view so that you can see the report shown here:

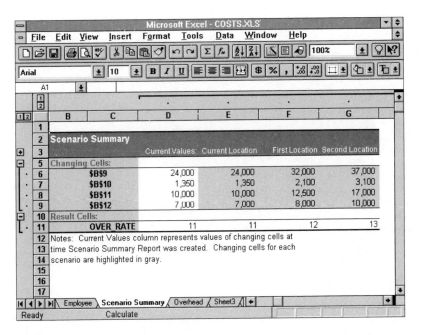

As you can see, Scenario Manager displays the report in outline format so that you can easily hide or unhide rows and columns.

5. If you want a printed copy of the report, click the Print button. Then save both workbooks.

You now have a completed project estimate that takes into account your overhead costs as well as the direct costs associated with the project. You also have a means of assessing the impact of varying overhead costs. You can easily set up scenarios to examine the effects of other changes, such as salary increases.

As we said at the beginning of the chapter, you can adapt this set of worksheets in many ways to help you quickly assemble bids. You can also use versions of these worksheets for such tasks as comparing the cost of doing projects in-house with estimates that you receive from vendors. And once you have set up a lookup table such as the employee information table, you can link it to worksheets that perform a variety of other personnel-related calculations.

Time-Saving Techniques

What you will learn...

Use patterns to accentuate cells

Put borders around all the cells in a range

Outline ranges to create discrete sections

Biosphere Office Products
13478 S.W. 88th St.
Bellevue, WA 98111

ORDER DATE	INVOICE NUMBER

SHIP DATE	PO NUMBER

SOLD TO	SHIP TO

SOLD BY	TERMS	SHIP VIA	FREIGHT TERMS

Item #	Qty.	Part #	Description	Unit Cost	Extended Cost
				Total	
				Tax	
				Shipping/Handling	
				Amount Due	

[Transfer]

Create a button to make running a macro easier

Use a macro to transfer key data to another worksheet

In this final chapter, we discuss techniques that can greatly increase your efficiency by automating some of the routine tasks associated with setting up worksheets. First, we show you how to assign a name to combinations of formatting so that you can apply all the formatting simply by selecting the name. Then we tackle macros. Once you see how easy it is to record keystrokes as macros in Excel, even those of you whose palms get sweaty at the thought of having to deal with something as "techie" as a macro programming language will begin thinking of ways to put macros to use.

The example for this chapter is an invoice. In Chapter 3, we said we would show you a way to avoid having to manually input data into lists such as invoice logs. The key to streamlining the data-input process is to generate forms like invoices in Excel and then use a macro to make Excel do the work of transferring the data from the invoices to the invoice log.

Setting Up an Invoice

The invoice we are going to create in this chapter is shown on the previous page. Take a quick look to get oriented, and then let's set up the invoice worksheet:

1. If you have any workbooks open, close them. Open a new workbook and save it in the EXCEL\EXAMPLES directory as INVOICE.XLS.

2. Make the following entries in the indicated cells, using the capitalization shown:

Cell	Entry
F1	ORDER DATE
G1	INVOICE NUMBER
F4	SHIP DATE
G4	PO NUMBER
D7	SOLD TO
F7	SHIP TO
A13	SOLD BY
D13	TERMS
F13	SHIP VIA
G13	FREIGHT TERMS
A15	Item #
B15	Qty.

C15	Part #
D15	Description
F15	Unit Cost
G15	Extended Cost
F30	Total
F31	Tax
F32	Shipping/Handling
F34	Amount Due

3. Choose Column and then Width from the Format menu and adjust the column widths as follows:

A, B, C	6
D, F, G	18
E	1

4. Apply the Bold style to A13, D13, F13:G13, and F30:F34.

5. Center the entries in the range A15:G15.

6. Right-align cell D7 and the range F30:F34.

7. Apply the m/d/yy date format to cells F2 and F5.

8. Finally, apply the Currency format to the ranges F16:F29 and G16:G34.

Using Named Styles

As you know, to apply a style to a selected cell or range, you can click the appropriate button, or you can choose the Cells command from the Format menu, click the Font tab, and set the font, style, and size options. On page 50, we discussed copying styles using the Format Painter button. Here we'll take a quick look at another formatting shortcut: named styles.

Once you apply a combination of formatting to a particular cell or range, you can save that combination as a named style and then apply that combination of formatting to other ranges simply by selecting the name. Try out this feature by following these steps:

1. Select cell F1 and click the Bold button.

Changing a cell's background pattern

2. Choose Cells from the Format menu and click the Patterns tab to display these options:

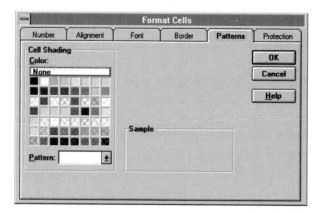

3. Click the down arrow to the right of the Pattern edit box to display a palette of patterns and colors. Select the third pattern in the first row and click OK. As you can see here, the cell's background is now shaded with the selected pattern:

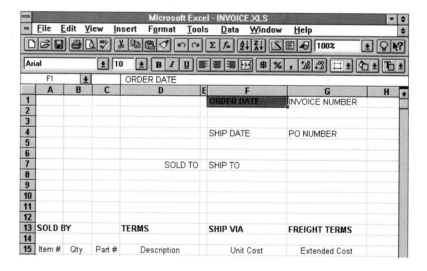

Next we'll create a named style for this combination of formatting:

Assigning a name

1. With cell F1 still selected, choose Style from the Format menu. Excel displays this dialog box:

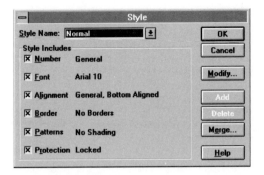

2. In the Style Name edit box, type *Heading 1*.

3. Click the Add button to save the formatting of the selected cell under the name Heading 1, and then click OK.

4. Select cell G1 and choose Style from the Format menu. Click the down arrow to the right of the Style Name edit box, select Heading 1 from the drop-down list, and click OK. The entry in G1 is now bold, and its background is shaded.

Applying a named style

Now let's add a Style box to the Formatting toolbar so that we can use the button to apply the Heading 1 style to a few of the other headings in the worksheet:

1. Choose Toolbars from the View menu and click the Customize button to display the Customize dialog box. In the Categories section, select Text Formatting to display the buttons used to format text:

Adding a button to a toolbar

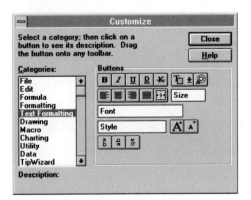

Modifying named styles

To change a named style, select a cell to which you have applied the style and choose Style from the Format menu. Click the Modify button to display the Format Cells dialog box. Make the changes and then click OK twice. Excel redefines the named style to incorporate the new formatting and changes the cells to which you have applied that style.

2. Drag the Style box to the Formatting toolbar between the Font Size and Bold buttons. When you release the mouse button, Excel adds the Style box to the toolbar and moves the Bold and subsequent buttons to the right.

Resizing toolbar boxes

3. So that all the buttons fit on the toolbar, resize the Font, Font Size, and Style boxes. (Click a box to select it, move the pointer over the box's frame, and when the pointer changes to opposing arrows, drag the pointer to reduce the size of the box.)

4. Click the Close button to return to your worksheet, where the toolbar now looks like this:

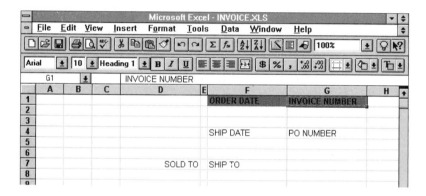

Now use the Style box to apply the Heading 1 style:

1. Select cell D7, hold down the Ctrl key, and select cell F7. Then click the down arrow to the right of the Style box to display a list of the named styles you have defined for this worksheet.

2. Click Heading 1 to apply its combination of styles.

3. Repeat steps 1 and 2 for the range F4:G4. Here are the results:

Deleting named styles

To delete a named style, select a cell to which you have applied the style and then choose the Style command from the Format menu. Select the style from the Style Name list, click the Delete button, and then click OK.

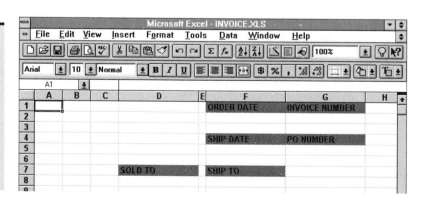

4. Click the Save button to save the work you have done so far.

As you can see, named styles are a convenient way of duplicating formatting you have defined for one part of your worksheet in other parts. Another important shortcut technique is to create a macro to apply frequently used styles or formats. We'll try this technique in the next section.

Creating Macros

An Excel macro is a set of instructions. When you run a macro, Excel moves sequentially through the instructions, doing whatever it is told to do. The instructions, called *statements*, are written on a macro sheet in the Visual Basic language. For example, this Visual Basic statement

=Range("F2").Select

tells Excel to select cell F2 on the active sheet. The first part of the statement identifies the place of action and the second part states the type of action.

To make it easy for new users to create macros right away, Excel has a macro recorder with which you can record a series of keystrokes and commands as a macro. Excel takes care of translating the keystrokes and commands into the Visual Basic language and writing them on a macro sheet. Excel gives this macro sheet the name Module followed by a number, such as Module1.

You assign the macro a name so that you can "play it back" by choosing Macro from the Tools menu, selecting the macro's name in the Macro dialog box, and clicking the Run button. You can also designate a shortcut key combination that you can press to run the macro. You can even link the macro to a "button" that you create on the worksheet so that you can run the macro by clicking the button.

Our discussion of macros will be necessarily brief and is not intended to make you an instant Excel macro expert. The idea is to get you thinking about whether tasks you perform routinely could be more efficiently carried out with macros and to give you enough information to explore the topic further

Visual Basic statements

The macro recorder

Visual Basic

The Visual Basic language has been added to Excel 5 to allow you to automate your work with user-defined macros. You can also use Visual Basic to build complex procedures that define menus, dialog boxes, messages, and buttons. Skilled Visual Basic programmers can even create custom versions of Excel that look like totally different applications. The *Visual Basic User's Guide* has general guidelines and examples to assist you in learning how to use this powerful programming language.

on your own. We start by showing you how to record a macro. Next, we take a look at the macro sheet and the process by which you create macros from scratch. Then we assign a macro to a button. Finally, we examine a macro that transfers information from a filled-out invoice to an invoice log.

Recording Macros

To resemble the invoice at the beginning of the chapter, the invoice now on your screen needs borders around several ranges. We will use the Border button on the toolbar for the purpose of creating an Outline macro, like this:

The Outline macro

1. Select A8:D11, the first range you want to outline.

Turning on the macro recorder

2. Turn on the macro recorder by choosing Record Macro from the Tools menu and then Record New Macro from the sub-menu. Excel displays this dialog box:

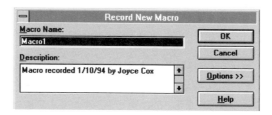

3. Type *Outline* as the name of the macro, and click Options to expand the dialog box like this:

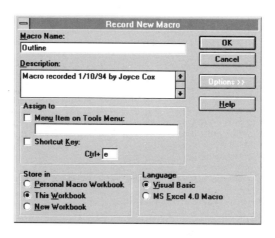

Assigning a shortcut key combination

4. To be able to run the macro simply by pressing Ctrl+o, click the Shortcut Key option, replace the *e* in the Ctrl+ edit box with *o*, and click OK. Excel displays the Stop Macro button

in the top right corner of your worksheet and begins recording. From now until you turn off the recorder, Excel records every action you take.

5. Click the down arrow to the right of the Border button and select the thickest Outline button (the bottom right button).

6. Click the Stop Macro button to stop recording.

Turning off the macro recorder

Excel places the macro on a sheet called Module1 and inserts the sheet after the last sheet in the workbook. Let's look at the Module1 sheet and its macro:

1. Use the tab-scrolling buttons to display the Module1 tab and click it. Excel displays the macro and the Visual Basic toolbar.

Viewing Module1

2. Drag the Visual Basic toolbar up and to the left so that it arranges itself under the Formatting toolbar and your screen looks like this:

```
' Outline Macro
' Macro recorded 1/10/94 by Joyce Cox

' Keyboard Shortcut: Ctrl+o

Sub Outline()
    Selection.Borders(xlLeft).LineStyle = xlNone
    Selection.Borders(xlRight).LineStyle = xlNone
    Selection.Borders(xlTop).LineStyle = xlNone
    Selection.Borders(xlBottom).LineStyle = xlNone
    Selection.BorderAround Weight:=xlMedium, ColorIndex:=xlAutomatic
End Sub
```

Excel creates a header for the macro, which includes the macro name, the date the macro was recorded, who recorded the macro, and the shortcut key combination. The macro is color-coded to distinguish comments (the heading), procedures (Sub, End Sub), and statements (the macro code). The five lines of code shows the different options for defining a

Smart recorder

If you cancel an action, or click Cancel in a dialog box while Excel is recording a macro, the action is not recorded. If you Undo an action, Excel records both the action and the Undo command.

border. The first four lines indicate the border options you did not select, and the fifth line indicates the line weight and color for the option (BorderAround) you did select.

The Visual Basic toolbar

As you have seen, Excel automatically displays the Visual Basic toolbar when you move to a macro sheet. If you use ToolTips to explore this toolbar, you'll see that the five middle buttons are used to work directly with the macro, and the others are used to edit and debug the code. In addition, Excel has changed the menu bar to provide the commands needed for working with macros. Use the Help button if you want to find out what the commands do.

Let's return to Sheet1 and create a second macro called Border to put a thick border around each cell in a selected range. You can't use the Border button for this purpose because the button puts a thin border around each cell. To create a thick border, you must choose Cells from the Format menu, click the Border tab, select the border style, click the Left, Right, Top, and Bottom options, and click OK. This set of steps is an ideal candidate for a simple recorded macro, so let's get to work:

The Border macro

1. Click the tab-scrolling buttons so that you can click the Sheet1 tab and display the invoice on your screen.

2. Select F1:G2 and turn on the recorder by choosing Record Macro and then Record New Macro from the Tools menu.

3. In the Record New Macro dialog box, type *Border* as the name of the macro, click Options, and specify Ctrl+b as the shortcut key. Then click OK.

4. Choose Cells from the Format menu and click the Border tab. In the Style section, select the third line in the left column. In the Border section, click the Left, Right, Top, and Bottom boxes and then click OK.

5. Click the Stop Macro button to stop recording.

Let's look at how Excel has written the second macro:

1. Click the tab-scrolling buttons and display the Module1 sheet by clicking its tab.

Macro libraries

You might want to build a library of general-purpose macros in a separate workbook file. Assign the file a filename such as MACLIB.XLS and open that workbook whenever you want to access the macros it contains. (For example, you might want to copy the Outline and Border macros to a workbook for use with other worksheet projects.)

2. Scroll through the sheet. Excel has placed the second macro below the first. Notice the similarity in the macros' layouts.

3. When you finish, redisplay Sheet1.

Running Macros

Now you are ready to test these two macros on the invoice. Because you have assigned shortcut keys to the macros, you can run them simply by pressing Ctrl+b or Ctrl+o from the keyboard. Here goes:

1. Select F4:G5 and press Ctrl+b. Excel puts a border around each cell in the range.

Using the shortcut key
combinations

2. Now select F8:G11 and press Ctrl+o. Excel puts a border around the perimeter of the selected range. Press Ctrl+Home so that you can see these results:

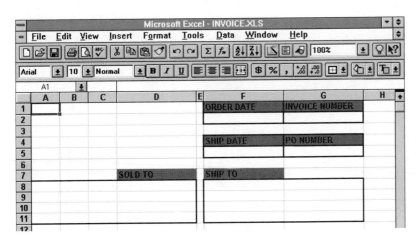

Both macros are working correctly, so let's use them to outline some more ranges:

1. Select A13:C14 and press Ctrl+o.

2. Select the following ranges in turn and press Ctrl+o after each selection:

D13:E14	B16:B29
F13:F14	C16:C29
G13:G14	D16:E29
D15:E15	F16:F29
A16:A29	G16:G29

Macro availability

A macro is available for use in either of two situations: when you open the workbook in which the macro is stored, or when you assign a macro to a custom button on a toolbar. See the tip on page 153 for more information.

3. Select the following cells or ranges in turn and press Ctrl+b after each selection:

D7   F15:G15
F7   G30:G32
A15:C15   G34

Turning off grid lines

4. To make the borders stand out, choose Options from the Tools menu, display the View tab, deselect the Gridlines option (there should be no X in its check box), and click OK.

5. Click the Print Preview button on the Standard toolbar to see the results:

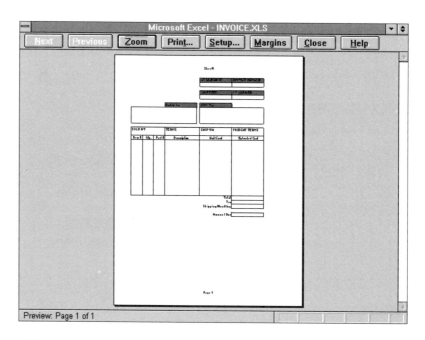

6. Click the Close button, and then click Save to preserve the work you have done so far.

A thorough examination of Excel's macro capabilities is beyond the scope of this book. Suffice it to say that macro instructions exist for just about every worksheet task you can **Help with macros** perform. The Excel Help system includes information about macros and Visual Basic, so to learn more about macros in general and about specific macro instructions, read the Macros and Visual Basic Reference topics in Help.

Defining Macros from Scratch

You've probably noticed the blank hole in the top left corner of the invoice. Let's create a simple macro that will insert a company name and address in this area. In the process, you'll learn a little more about the Visual Basic language.

Before we get going, here are a few pointers about working in a macro sheet. Basically, typing a macro is like working with a simple word processor or text editor. You use the Enter key to move to the next line, and you can use all the usual techniques to edit your work. You can even cut, copy, and paste text. If you make a mistake when typing macro code, Excel displays the line in red, highlights the error's location, and displays a message describing the type of error. If you are unsure of how to correct the error, click the Help button; otherwise, click OK and make the necessary changes.

Now let's get going:

1. Double-click the Sheet1 tab and rename the sheet as Invoice.

The Letterhead macro

2. Move to the Module1 sheet and click an insertion point on the line immediately below the last macro.

3. To enter the company name and address, type the macro instructions shown below just as you see them:

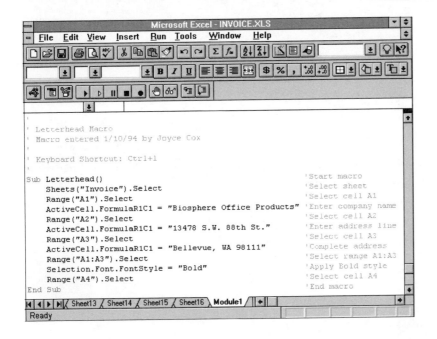

You may want to substitute your own company's name and address. You don't have to type the comments, which explain the action of each instruction.

4. To assign a shortcut key to the macro, choose Macro from the Tools menu to display the Macro dialog box:

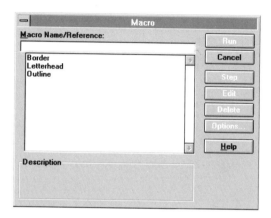

5. Select Letterhead and click Options to display this dialog box:

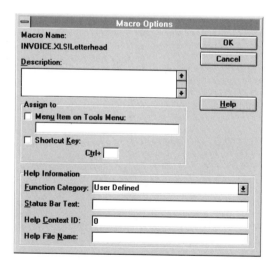

Halting macros

You can halt a running macro's progress at any point by simply clicking the Esc button. Excel displays a dialog box telling you at what cell it stopped the macro. You can then proceed by clicking the Halt, Step, Continue, or Goto buttons.

6. Click the Shortcut Key option, type *l* in the Ctrl+ edit box, click OK, and then click the Close button to close the Macro dialog box.

7. Save your work by clicking the Save button.

Now let's test the new macro:

1. Click an insertion point anywhere within the Letterhead macro and click the Run Macro button on the Visual Basic toolbar.

   Excel moves to the Invoice sheet and inserts the letterhead text. This is the result:

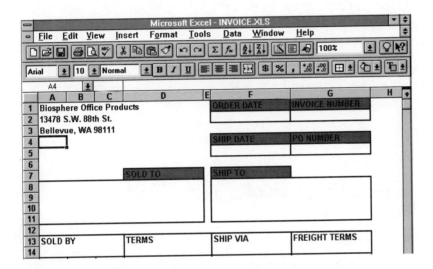

   If the macro doesn't work, follow these steps:

1. Choose Macro from the Tools menu to display the Macro dialog box.

2. Select Letterhead and click the Edit button. Excel takes you to Module1. Make the necessary changes so that your macro looks exactly like the one on page 147. Then try running the macro again.

Importing graphics

To create a really fancy letterhead, you can import a graphic that has been created in a graphics program. Choose Picture from the Insert menu to display the Picture dialog box, where you can select the graphics file you want to import. You can then size the graphic and position it anywhere on the worksheet by dragging it.

Excel supports object linking and embedding (OLE), which creates a conduit between two applications. You can use OLE to exchange data between Excel documents or between an Excel worksheet and a document created in another application. (Both applications must support OLE.) For example, to embed a Paintbrush graphic in a worksheet, choose Object from Excel's Insert menu to display a list of applications from which you can embed objects. Double-click Paintbrush Picture to open a Paintbrush window, where you can create the graphic. When you finish, choose Exit And Return To *Workbook* to embed the graphic object in the Excel worksheet, clicking Yes to update the object. If you want to change the graphic later, all you have to do is double-click the embedded object to open a Paintbrush window within Excel.

Logging Invoice Data with a Macro

You now know enough about macros to follow along as we create one that will take the information you enter in the invoice and record it in an invoice log. This macro can be adapted for many uses. For example, you could use the techniques you learned while creating the invoice to develop a contacts template. You could then adapt the macro to pull information about each new client you work with into a name and address list. Or you might want to create an expense-report template and adapt the macro to record expenses in a reimbursement summary.

Before we can work on the macro, we need to create the invoice log sheet, so let's get started.

Setting Up an Invoice Log

For demonstration purposes, we'll keep this log very simple. Follow these steps:

1. Double-click the Sheet2 tab and rename it as Log.

2. Make the following entries in the indicated cells on the new worksheet:

A1	INVOICE LOG
A3	Date
B3	Invoice Number
C3	Salesperson
D3	Amount of Sale

3. Select A1:D3 and click the Bold button. Then select A1:D1 and click the Center Across Columns button.

4. Adjust the column widths so that you can see all the entries.

5. Format column A with the m/d/yy date format and format column D with the currency format.

Designating the end of a worksheet

6. We want Excel to append new invoices to the end of the invoice log, so select cell A4, choose Name and then Define from the Insert menu, type the name *END*, and click OK to assign that name. Then press Ctrl+Home to move to the top of the worksheet, which looks like this:

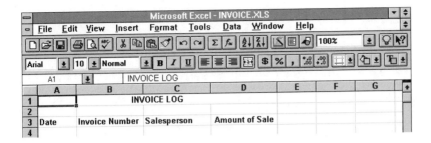

7. Return to the Invoice worksheet and assign the following names to the specified cells:

F2   ORDER_DATE
G2   INVOICE_NUMBER
A14   SOLD_BY
G34   AMOUNT_DUE

8. Click the Save button to save the workbook.

Creating the Invoice_Log Macro

That's it for setting up the log. Now let's create the macro:

1. Display the Module1 sheet and click an insertion point at the beginning of the line after the last macro. Enter the following macro called Invoice_Log. (We've moved the Visual Basic toolbar so that you can see the entire macro.)

The Invoice_Log macro

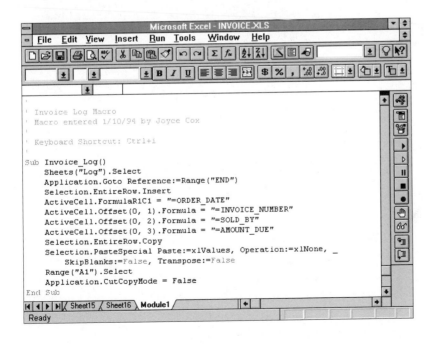

2. Assign a shortcut key to the macro by choosing Macro from the Tools menu. With Invoice_Log selected in the Macro dialog box, click the Options button, click Shortcut Key, type the letter *i* in the Ctrl+ edit box, click OK, and then click the Close button.

3. Click the Save button to save the macro.

Understanding the macro code

To understand what the macro is doing, look at the Invoice_ Log macro and review the following explanation, starting with the *Sheets("Log").Select* line:

Line 1:	Select the Log sheet
Line 2:	Move to the cell named END
Line 3:	Insert a row, moving the named cell down one row
Line 4:	Place the data from the cell named ORDER_DATE into the current cell (ActiveCell)
Line 5:	From the current cell (ActiveCell), move (Offset) to the same row (0) and one column to the right (1). Insert the formula =INVOICE_NUMBER
Line 6:	From the current cell (ActiveCell), move (Offset) to the same row (0) and two columns to the right (2). Insert the formula =SOLD_BY
Line 7:	From the current cell (ActiveCell), move (Offset) to the same row (0) and three columns to the right (3). Insert the formula =AMOUNT_DUE

The next two lines of the macro replace the formulas with their values. This way, when the information in the Invoice sheet changes, the information in these cells will not change.

Line 8:	Selects the row and copies its contents
Line 9:	Paste only the values back into the row, replacing the formulas. (The underscore at the end of the line means that the code continues on the next line.)

The last two lines complete the macro.

Line 10:   Select cell A1
Line 11:   End the Copy/Paste process

Running the Macro

Now for the acid test. We'll make a few entries in the Invoice worksheet and then run the macro. Here goes:

1. In the Invoice worksheet, make the following entries in the indicated cells:

F2   9/9/94
G2   5234AA
A14   Karnov, Peter
G34   54687

2. Press Ctrl+i. If you have entered the macro correctly, Excel transfers the information you entered in the invoice to the log, as shown here:

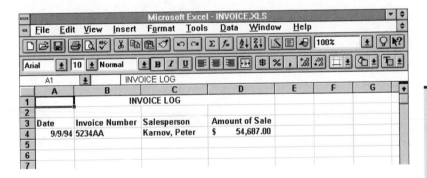

You might want to enter new values in the Invoice sheet and then press Ctrl+i to run the macro again to see how Excel appends the information from successive invoices to the Invoice Log.

Assigning Macros to Buttons

As we mentioned earlier, you can assign a macro to a button on the worksheet and run the macro simply by clicking the button. Buttons provide instant access to your macros and serve as a graphic reminder of a macro's availability. In this

Button macros

You can assign a macro to an unused toolbar button and then display the button on a toolbar. Choose the Toolbar command from the View menu and select the Custom category to display a set of buttons that currently have no macro assigned to them. Click a button and drag it to the desired toolbar. When Excel displays the Assign Macro dialog box, select a macro for the button and click OK. Then whenever you want to run the macro, you can simply click the button on the toolbar.

section, we'll use the Create Button button to create a button that represents the Invoice_Log macro. Follow these steps:

1. Change the invoice entries in the Invoice sheet as follows, and then press Ctrl+Home:

F2	10/12/94
G2	5784AA
A14	Karnov, Peter
G34	32621

2. Click the Drawing button to display the floating Drawing toolbar.

3. Click the Create Button button on the Drawing toolbar, and draw a box to the left of Amount Due at the bottom of the invoice. (Don't worry about the exact size; you can adjust the button later.) Excel displays the Assign Macro dialog box with a list of available macros:

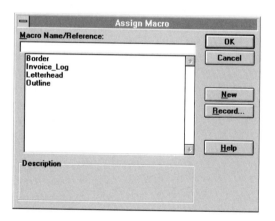

4. Select Invoice_Log and click OK.

5. Type *Transfer* as the label for the button, and click anywhere on the worksheet to deselect the button.

6. If you need to resize the button, hold down the Ctrl key and click the button. Then grab any of its handles, and reshape it. When you've finished, the button should look like this:

Graphic macro buttons

You can assign macros to any graphic object you create—even a line or an edit box. Just select the object and choose Assign Macro from the Tools menu. When Excel displays the Assign Macro dialog box, select a macro and click OK. The next time you click the object, Excel runs the macro.

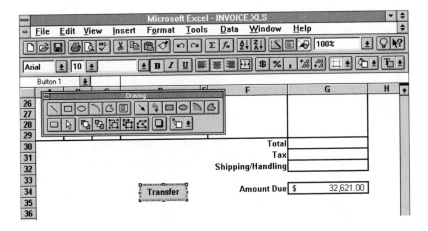

7. Click anywhere in the sheet to clear the button handles, and then click the box containing the hyphen in the top left corner of the Drawing toolbar's title bar to remove the toolbar.

Now we'll test the button:

1. Click the Transfer button. Excel executes the Invoice_Log macro and adds the new invoice information to the log, which now looks like this:

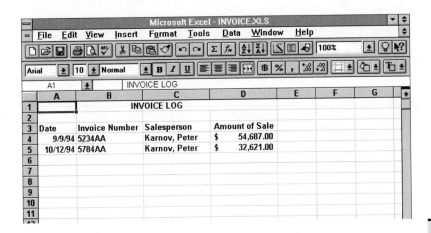

The button is a permanent part of the Invoice worksheet. If you need to change or delete it, right-click the button and choose the appropriate command from its shortcut menu.

If the Macro Doesn't Work

How Excel responds if it encounters an error in a macro depends on the type of error. It might stop, move to the macro sheet, select the line with the error, and display a message

Macro button changes

If you need to assign a different macro to a button, use the Selection button on the Drawing toolbar to select the button, or hold down the Ctrl key and click the button. Then choose the Assign Macro command from the Tools menu, and select another macro.

defining the error. You can then click Help to display an explanation of the error or click OK to move directly to the code to correct the error. On the other hand, Excel might display a Macro Error message box explaining the error. You can then click End to end the macro; click Debug to move to a Debug window where you can attempt to resolve the problem; click Goto to move to the macro sheet with the offending line highlighted; or click Help.

The most likely cause of errors is typos. But if you can't see anything wrong, Excel offers ways to sleuth out the cause of the problem. On the Visual Basic toolbar are four buttons for finding errors. We'll look briefly at three of these buttons: Toggle Breakpoint, Step Into, and Step Over.

You use the Toggle Breakpoint button when you want to view the results of a portion of the code to find out the cause of an error. When you click the Toggle Breakpoint button, Excel puts a breakpoint in the macro code. Then when you run the macro, Excel stops the procedure at the breakpoint and displays the Debug window, an example of which is shown here:

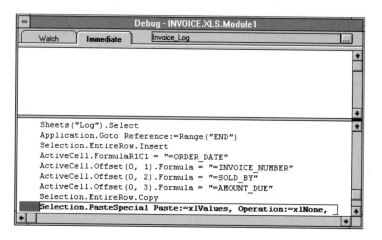

When you are ready to continue the macro, click the Resume button on the Visual Basic toolbar. Remove the breakpoint by clicking anywhere in the breakpoint line of code and clicking the Toggle Breakpoint button.

You can use both the Step Into and Step Over buttons to display the Debug window and step through the macro one line at a time. (Step Into also steps through "called" procedures, whereas Step Over skips these procedures.) These buttons allow you to see the macro in slow motion, increasing your chances of spotting errors. As you step through the macro, Excel places a box around the line that is being executed, as shown here:

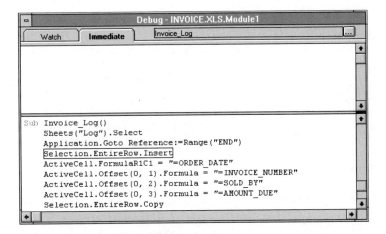

```
Debug - INVOICE.XLS.Module1

  Watch    Immediate    Invoice_Log                    [...]




Sub Invoice_Log()
    Sheets("Log").Select
    Application.Goto Reference:=Range("END")
    Selection.EntireRow.Insert
    ActiveCell.FormulaR1C1 = "=ORDER_DATE"
    ActiveCell.Offset(0, 1).Formula = "=INVOICE_NUMBER"
    ActiveCell.Offset(0, 2).Formula = "=SOLD_BY"
    ActiveCell.Offset(0, 3).Formula = "=AMOUNT_DUE"
    Selection.EntireRow.Copy
```

Click the Resume button when you finish stepping and want to complete the execution of the macro.

Well, that quick overview of macros winds up the book. You are now equipped with the tools you need to create some pretty sophisticated worksheets and should be familiar enough with Excel to explore the more complex features on your own.

Index

Other Quick Course® Books

Don't miss the other titles in our Quick Course® series! Quality books at the unbeatable price of $12.95!

A Quick Course in DOS 6

A Quick Course in DOS 5

A Quick Course in Windows 3.1

A Quick Course in Windows for Workgroups

A Quick Course in Word 6 for Windows

A Quick Course in Word 2 for Windows

A Quick Course in WordPerfect 6 for Windows

A Quick Course in WordPerfect 6 for DOS

A Quick Course in WordPerfect 5.1 for Windows

A Quick Course in WordPerfect 5.1 for DOS

A Quick Course in Lotus 1-2-3 Release 4 for Windows

A Quick Course in Quattro Pro for Windows

A Quick Course in Paradox for Windows

Plus many more...

For our latest catalog, call (800) 854-3344 or write to us at:

Online Press Inc.
14320 NE 21st Street, Suite 18
Bellevue, WA 98007